CHANGE YOUR THINKING

•

CHANGE YOUR LIFE

Learn to Live Your Best Life Possible

GLENN POVEROMO
DR. JESSIE POVEROMO

Contents

Preface

My motive for writing this book is to offer you a gift. It is my fervent wish that you will read this book and pay attention to your thoughts and feelings as you do so. By paying attention to your thoughts and feelings, you will develop a deeper understanding of the belief systems you have developed within your mind that have guided you toward your present station in life.

When I speak with audiences, I title my presentation, "A Program of Insight and Empowerment." I do not claim to know life's deepest secrets, nor do I pontificate about sure-fire ways to achieve success, fulfillment, and happiness. What I do best is offer you insights that, if you take the time to consider, will place your feet on the path toward empowerment. All journeys begin with the proverbial first step, and once you take the initial step upon the path, whatever you are seeking will begin to be revealed to you. The speed and ease of your revelations can be accelerated by your understanding of the power of your mind and how to effectively use this power to enhance your journey upon this planet.

When you consider the insights of anyone, three distinct outcomes become possible. One is that you will read all I have written and the contents of this text will resonate within you. You will employ the mental tools detailed within and make a complete transformation in your life. Nothing would make me happier than the privilege of helping to shape your life into a happy, interesting, and fulfilling journey.

A second possible outcome that could occur when you consider an insight is that many, or perhaps only a few, of the ideas contained within this book might open your mind to discovering new ideas that help you to live a happier and more fulfilling life. You can pick and choose ideas that ignite a spark of hope and empowerment within you and discard those that do not seem feasible in your personal paradigm of truth. Feel free to borrow any ideas that excite you and develop them further as your own.

The third possible outcome of considering the insight that another has offered to you is that you will totally disagree with everything that person has to say. This result will also serve to empower you, because by rejecting my ideas, you will be reinforcing within yourself the ideas and beliefs that work best for you. In all circumstances, the more intimately we know ourselves and what makes us function best, the more we become empowered to live our best lives possible.

As your life improves, you will project an aura and energy that those around you will notice and respond to. As your life becomes better, you will become capable of influencing those around you to have lives that are better, and they in turn can influence those around them to become better as well.

Please accept this gift and begin your quest toward living your best life possible.

One

Our Powerful Mind

When we learn that thoughts are truly choices, we learn that we are capable of choosing to live our best life possible...Think about that!

I am like many of you who are seeking ways to make life a richer and more fulfilling journey. If your experiences are similar to mine, you may have read dozens of books, attended countless lectures and seminars, listened to and watched an endless stream of CDs and DVDs, and tried numerous strategies to uncover that ever-elusive formula for success. Each time I employed a new technique and traveled a new path with the certainty that I had found my way, those same old patterns of self-doubt led to those same old patterns of self-sabotage and ultimately left me standing back on that proverbial "square one." I was living life by that powerful default system that said one step forward, two steps back. It was only when I slowed my seeking down and learned to be in the present that the obvious answers I had been searching for became a conscious part of my constitution. Relinquishing the stress and pain of constant seeking, as well as the financial investments, which had become quite steep, I arrived upon the two great insights that have transformed my life completely.

These two great insights are:

1. Thoughts are always choices.

2. Permanent and effective change does not come from actions; permanent and effective change comes from first changing our beliefs.

Once one learns to master these two simple concepts, life becomes the creation of design rather than creation by default. In other words, we gain control of our destiny by learning to use the power of our mind.

What is the meaning of life? It's whatever you believe it to be... Think about that!

You are where you are in life as the result of the thoughts you have been thinking. Many people believe that their status in life is the result of circumstance, but this is not entirely true. Although the circumstances that have occurred in your life, both those you have chosen and those that have been thrust upon you, do play an integral role in the development of your belief systems, the larger influence in their development is your perceptions of and responses toward these circumstances. In other words, it is not so much what has happened that forms your beliefs; where you are in life is the product of how you have *responded* to what has happened. Your responses are ultimately the result of your belief systems, which you began developing in your formative years. Your reaction to any stimulus is based upon what you have conditioned your mind to believe. If you are seeking to change a response to any stimulus, you must first change your belief. Before we delve more deeply into this concept, let's take a moment to discuss just how beliefs are formed.

Beliefs are thoughts we think over and over again that are charged with emotion.

Tribal Beliefs

Our most basic beliefs are taught to us by our primary caregivers. It is usually parents, siblings, relatives, clergy, etc.— the most prominent people in our lives—who have helped to create these beliefs. Their truths become our truths. We become a part of their religion; we share their concept of God's existence or nonexistence. We learn our responses to stress, our perceptions of right and wrong, and our attitude to just about everything from food to our favorite sports teams from them. These perceptions become embedded in our subconscious mind and become our truths. Anything outside of our belief system leaves us feeling uncomfortable. The most secure place for us to function is within our tribal belief system, even if that belief system is dysfunctional.

How Others Respond to Us

As our evolution continues, we begin to venture beyond our immediate sphere of influence and we encounter new influences that further shape our belief systems. Teachers, friends, classmates, coaches, and others present us with a wide array of ideas. We align ourselves with those who most comfortably match our paradigm of truth. Once we have entered their sphere of influence, we begin to expand our belief systems. This can help to shape either a positive or negative perception of self. For instance, a teacher who conveys to us that we are not smart, classmates who tell us we are not popular, and coaches who tell us our skills will never be good enough leave an indelible impression upon our psyche. If we allow ourselves to believe their perception of us, we will be left with feelings of self-doubt, inferiority, the inability to succeed, etc. We will respond to the stimulus of social situations with a cautious and limiting mind-set. These types of influences help to create negative "truths" that are not necessarily true. Conversely, the teacher who helps us to feel intelligent and creative, the classmates who respond to us with admiration and respect, and the coaches who help us to believe we can succeed help us to develop a belief that we will overcome the challenges that life brings our way.

Experiences

A major contributor to the development of our belief system is experience. Our thoughts of either *I can* or *I can't* are often the result of trial and error. When we encounter new and unfamiliar circumstances, our willingness to move forward or desire to shy away will be based upon our level of confidence that we are capable of succeeding. Our subconscious mind will quickly scan our memory banks for related experiences of the past, which will make us feel either comfortable or uncomfortable. The more comfortable we feel, the more thoughts of *I can* will fill our mind and permit us to try new things. Conversely, the more uncomfortable we feel, the more thoughts of *I can't* will fill our mind and we will choose not to try. The old adage, "Experience is our best teacher" bears a great deal of truth in the formation of our system of belief.

Our Intuitive Self

Beyond our immediate spheres of influence is the part of us that knows who we are and what to do through our intuition. We all have intuitive feelings that resonate within us regarding our responses to certain stimuli, and as we become more familiar with and trusting of these intuitive feelings, we shape beliefs that might be contrary to what we have been taught. These deep, intuitive feelings might take us beyond our comfort zone of truth, but we will understand from that deep part of ourselves that we must be true to our intuition. Our ability to tune in to our intuition might come to us naturally or might be developed over time. As we learn to trust and focus our awareness upon the instinctive or "gut" feelings of our body, the intuitive self becomes more influential in reshaping our belief system.

We do not outperform our beliefs; it's just the way it is.

Consider the following diagram, which indicates how our beliefs affect our performance:

<u>Live Your Best Life Possible</u>

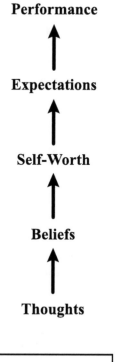

Performance

↑

Expectations

↑

Self-Worth

↑

Beliefs

↑

Thoughts

CHOICES

Our performance in any arena of life is really the product of our expectations, and our expectations are influenced by our feelings of self-worth. When someone harbors a belief that he or she is unworthy of succeeding at a task or accomplishing a goal (e.g., securing a job, performing in athletics, earning a diploma, finding a mate, etc.), then he or she will find a way to sabotage success because the expectation of the outcome is based upon the belief of not being good enough. Any success that does take place will eventually slip into failure because the belief system built by the individual will cause a feeling of discomfort. The end result will be the surrendering of the success that has been temporarily attained.

The same principle exists for those who have developed a system of belief that supports a feeling of self-worth, which tells them that they are in fact good enough and deserving of success. These individuals seem to experience constant "good luck" and project the image that everything goes their way. The real reason that these individuals are capable of accomplishing success is their expectation that they are deserving of success and good fortune.

Belief systems are built upon patterns of thought, those thoughts we think over and over again that are charged with emotion. When one learns to master one's thoughts, one learns to master one's life. This is why developing the skill of consciously choosing one's thoughts is the essential ingredient in creating one's best life possible.

If you believe you can't...you will fail.

If you believe you can...you will succeed.

<u>Confidence—The Key to Success:</u>

Many of us are reluctant to try something new simply because we lack the confidence that we will be successful. Rather than try and possibly fail, we create a plethora of "reasons" why we will not try, even though these "reasons" are in truth excuses we use to mask our fear both to ourselves and others. A lack of confidence gives rise to our inhibitions and creates self-imposed limits that prohibit us from living our best life possible. As we progress through life, our regrets of the past are not so much what we have done but what we failed to try.

The lack of confidence might be a sad truth that we have created for ourselves, but this truth can be transformed into a mind-set of confidence by understanding and mastering the power of the mind. The world of limitations that held us down can become a limitless world of discovery and fulfillment. We are all capable of using our minds to create our best life possible.

Two

Our mind is our most powerful tool. When we learn to use it correctly, we become empowered to create our best life possible.

The Place of Truth—
Our Subconscious Mind

Once we learn that our response to stimuli is based upon our deep-rooted beliefs, it is important to understand just where these beliefs live. When we understand the source, we are then capable of creating any belief systems we consciously choose.

To simplify our understanding, let us consider that we possess a mind divided into parts, plus a filtering system. One part of our mind is our active or conscious mind. This is the part that processes information, makes calculations, assesses data, makes choices, and so on. Our conscious mind is analogous to the processor of a computer. It responds to commands based upon the data that have been programmed into its hard drive.

Our subconscious mind is the place where the program is written and the data is stored. When we call upon our processor to make a calculation, it can only respond according to the information that has been programmed into it. If a program has been created that renders 2+2=5, then that will always be the answer derived whenever the equation presents itself, even though it is incorrect in reality. The same is true of our conscious, responsive mind. It will only respond to circumstances according to the thoughts we have created as our truths. Whatever we have programmed into our belief system through the thoughts we have conditioned our mind to think will become our truths. As a result, our actions are the product of our beliefs.

We also possess a filtering system; this is the figurative "space" between our conscious and subconscious minds. This filter is analogous to a "guard" whose job it is to watch over our deep-rooted beliefs and make sure that we respond to stimuli exactly as we have programmed our mind to believe we should, thus keeping us comfortable. This guard is powerful and not easily deceived. When we encounter a new idea or perception, our guard will quickly evaluate its merit and either dismiss or entertain it according to our feeling of comfort or discomfort. For every stimulus we experience, we have a reaction based upon our belief system. To understand how this works, think about how you would respond to the following stimuli:

- Bungee jumping

- Riding on the back of a fast motorcycle

- A night at the opera

- Handling snakes

- Flying in an airplane

- Being in a closed space

- Public speaking

For each of these stimuli, you will have an immediate response based upon your programmed belief system. Some might be an immediate yes, an immediate no, or a thought of maybe. Yet, however you respond, it will be based upon your programmed belief system. Should you take the time to dwell on the possibility of altering your perception of a stimulus and create a new response, your guard will do everything possible to sabotage your efforts. It holds fast to the job description it has been born to do: guard your established beliefs and keep you in your comfort zone, even if your comfort zone makes you feel negative. Change is not a welcomed guest in the domain of our beliefs. That is the limiting news. The good news, however, is that change is always possible.

Let's take a moment to review a few key points:

- All of life is based on what we believe it to be.

- Beliefs are thoughts we think over and over again that are charged with emotion.

- Our conscious mind responds to stimuli based upon the belief system we have programmed into our subconscious mind.

- Our filtering system, or "guard," evaluates all stimuli and decides which to entertain and which to discard.

- Change is always possible.

- Change begins first in the mind.

Just the thought of Grandma's pasta makes my mouth water!

More to Know about the Subconscious Mind

Understanding the power and the function of the subconscious mind is the key to transformation. Keeping in mind that your subconscious mind is the source of your belief system and dictates how you respond to stimuli, there are a few more things to know and understand about this powerful part of your mind. Most prominent is the fact that the subconscious mind is literal; it does not discriminate between what is imagined and what is real, nor does it judge. It responds solely to what you have programmed it to believe. For example, have you ever experienced a nightmare? What do you notice about your body upon waking? You might be shivering or sweating, or perhaps find yourself curled into the fetal position. Another example of how the subconscious mind is literal is how you respond to the thought of your favorite meal. The mere thought of it might make you salivate even though the meal is nowhere in sight. In both cases, even though the actual circumstances are imagined, the responses are real. Why is this so? It is because your subconscious mind was given a stimulus and instructed your body to respond in a preprogrammed way.

Another fact to consider about the subconscious mind is that it is malleable; it can be shaped and formed into new patterns of thought and belief. Once these thoughts and beliefs are securely in place, it will then respond to stimuli based on how it has been reprogrammed. Your belief system can be transformed from an "I can't" response to that of "I can."

Is it really possible to consciously reprogram our subconscious mind? Is it really possible to consciously create a new belief system? Is it really possible for us to take control of the outcomes in our life? The answer is a simple: yes, it is!

We will not outperform our beliefs. If we believe we can't, we'll find a way to fail. If we believe we can, we'll find a way to succeed. The way to improve our performance is to improve the patterns of our thinking!

As previously stated, how we perform in life is based upon the programs we have established in our mind through the patterns of thought we have instructed our mind to think. These patterned beliefs are automatic thoughts—thoughts that we are accustomed to thinking about ourselves that pop into our heads and make us feel a certain way about ourselves. An automatic thought can run through our minds, sometimes so quickly that we don't even realize it is there. After the thought has entered our minds, we experience an emotion. An example would be two students of equal intelligence who have different patterns of belief regarding their performance on exams. Student A has programmed her mind to expect no less than 90 percent on any exam she takes. Her automatic thoughts are, *I am a good student; I am a focused test taker.* After thinking these thoughts, she may feel confident and determined. If she receives a score below her believed level of performance, she will work harder to be sure to achieve a score on her next exam that will raise her average to 90 percent. Student B, although equal in intelligence, has programmed her mind to believe that she is only capable of achieving a grade in the low 80s. Her automatic thoughts are, *I am a poor test taker; I can't achieve anything more than a B-*, and she believes that she is incapable of scoring in the 90s. As a result, she may feel defeated and inadequate.

Many automatic thoughts are actually distorted, meaning they are not entirely accurate; they are programmed "truths" that are not necessarily true. People engage in different types of distortions, but they can all have the effect of making people feel badly about themselves or their performance. Should Student B receive a score of 90 percent or higher, she will likely tell herself that she was just lucky this time and be very uncomfortable with her grade. She will be apt to score much lower on her next exam; her mind will find ways to "screw up" because she needs to return to the comfort zone of her beliefs. If we consider ourselves failures, then we will find ways to sabotage our success; we become more comfortable failing than succeeding. The converse is true of those who have programmed their minds to succeed. To them, failure is not an option, and they will remain uncomfortable until they find a way to succeed. Think of all the "I can'ts" that exist in your life. If you take a moment to examine each one, you will discover that they are the result of the patterns of thinking, or the automatic thoughts you have created in your mind. What would be the effect of changing these patterns of thinking? Take a minute to evaluate whether the thoughts you are having are truly accurate or if you have just become so accustomed to thinking them that they are second nature to you now. If you wish to transform your performance to one of "I can" what you must do is transform the pattern of thinking you have created in your subconscious mind. Is this possible? It most certainly is!

Mental Exercise:

Create three columns. Label them A, B, and C.

In column A, make a list of the most prominent "I can'ts" that you use in your life. Examine each one carefully.

In column B, place a T next to each "I can't" that is true. Place an E next to each "I can't" that is an excuse you use to rationalize your failure to perform in a more proficient fashion.

In column C, write ways you can transform the "I can'ts" to "I cans." As you make these transformations, cross out the "I can'ts" that you've eliminated and continue to return to those that still exist.

Your Mental Exercise(s):

Three

Tools for the Mind

Our mind is our most powerful tool; once we learn to use it properly, we can create an amazing reality!

The ease with which any job is performed is based upon the tools that are available and the knowledge of how to use these tools. Imagine that you have decided to build a home and asked an expert to deliver to your building site the tools that will help you construct your home in the most efficient way possible. You would likely be staring at a vast array of tools and devices that the expert has provided for you. Based upon your expertise, there will be tools that you are familiar with and perhaps some that are unfamiliar to you. However, the bottom line is quite obvious. The more familiar you become with each tool, the greater your understanding of what each is capable of doing; the more skilled you become through practice, the more valuable each becomes in the construction of your home. The level of expertise you develop in using your tools will have a direct impact on the outcome of the time spent and the quality of what you have built.

There are mental tools available that you can use to build a system of beliefs that offers you control of the outcomes of your life. The more familiar and skilled you become with each mental tool, the more control you will have in creating whatever you desire.

Another Point of View

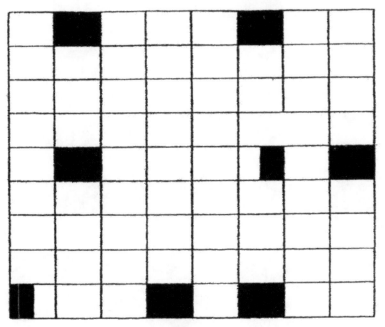

Can you discover this secret word?

Four

When we learn to actively choose our thoughts, we learn to actively choose our destiny...simple stuff.

<u>*Tool #1 Perception*</u>

If you've discovered the "secret" word, you will have seen the word *laugh*. In order to see the word, you needed to shift the paper into a different position, or another point of view. After you've seen it from this angle, you can see it from any direction that you choose. Had you not shifted your point of view, you would likely not have been able to see the word that has existed there the entire time. This is a metaphor for the way our mind works.

If we seek to make transformations in our life, we need to understand that if we think and perceive in the same patterns, if we maintain the same routines and rituals, we are not likely to make the transformation that we desire in our mind. In order to make changes in the way we think, we must make changes in the way we are looking at things.

A thought to consider is that we define ourselves, not by circumstances, but by how we *respond* to circumstances. We cannot control the force of a hurricane or the momentous force of an earthquake, but we can control how we respond during the occurrence of the event and we can control how we respond to the aftermath. How we respond will be the result of our perception. Some people will respond with utter despair and helplessness over their losses, while others who have experienced the same losses will set their minds in motion to find ways to create a new beginning. How one responds is based upon his or her perception. The good news is that even if one's original response is one of helplessness and despair, it can be transitioned into a perspective of a new beginning. Sometimes simply asking yourself, "Is there another way that I can look at this situation?" can be helpful. If not, choose a person in your life who you believe is a rational thinker and ask yourself how he or she might look at the situation. Sometimes getting out of your own perception and into someone else's can give you a whole new perspective. Those who have experienced the hurricane can choose to focus on the devastation, or they can choose to focus on alternative ways of viewing the same tragedy: "Even though the situation is terrible, my family is okay, I am still alive, I have people around me to help, etc." It becomes a matter of choosing thoughts that focus on the solution rather than thoughts that focus on the loss. Both ways of thinking will influence the outcomes of the challenge that has presented itself.

A good friend of mine related a story of something that happened to him that exemplifies the power of perception. He had begun a new business venture that was not bringing him much profit at the time of this occurrence. He was managing to pay his bills and was barely keeping his head above water. He had seen a product on the Internet that he felt would help him improve his productivity and sent a check for $1,500 toward that purpose. It did not take him long to realize that he had been scammed and his money was lost. He could have responded in any number of ways. Here is what he told me about his response:

"I could have been bitter and focused on the money that was lost or stolen from me. I could have focused my attention on how rotten this was and made myself sick over the incident. I realized that thinking in this direction would only make matters worse. The money was gone, and thinking about it wouldn't help me move forward. So I just chalked it up to experience and decided to move on. I also thought that if this person who cheated me needed the money so badly, then maybe it could help him in some way."

He told me the story with a smile on his face and then moved the conversation toward how he was planning to succeed. He chose a perception that focused not on what he had lost, but on what he had learned and what he had to gain. His business is now thriving, and he is continuously finding ways to expand it to even larger proportions.

Another example of how perception can change performance is the story of Eric, a former student of mine. From the moment Eric entered my class, he responded to me with an oppositional attitude. He was often rude, uncooperative, and disruptive. The very first day of class, I had to remove him and send him to the principal's office. In time, my patience began to wane, and I started responding to him with the same adversarial attitude that he had exhibited toward me. Each day of class was filled with tension. One day, I had Eric eat lunch with me in the classroom, since his behavior was so inappropriate that I would not allow him to play with his classmates during recess. Somewhere in that moment, I said something to him that opened a portal in his defenses, and he began to describe the hurt that was filling his consciousness. I listened patiently and without judgment. I cannot recall the exact dialogue that was exchanged, but I do recall that it opened a door to respect between us. We shared a moment of trust and understanding, and it was in this moment that an entirely new perception was created. The result of this new perception was a completely different attitude and pattern of behavior for us both. From that moment, Eric and I were partners rather than adversaries, and the entire spirit of our class changed from one of tension to one of happiness. All it took for this to occur was a shift in perspective.

Study the diagram below to see how a simple shift in perception can alter the outcome of one's life.

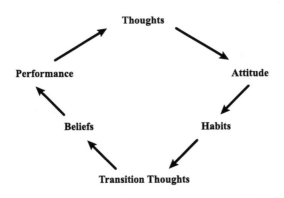

The above diagram indicates that as you change your thoughts, your attitude and your habits will follow. This in turn will create new patterns in thinking, or transition thoughts, which will take hold of your consciousness. As your thoughts transition, you begin to shape new beliefs. As you create new beliefs, you create new ways of performing and finally new outcomes.

Here is another example of how this actually works:

Fenton was a very large and powerful high school football player. There was little doubt in his or anyone's mind that he would one day play football at a major university and eventually secure a career in the National Football League. It seemed to be a given to everyone, including Fenton, that his career path had been secured from the time he entered the seventh grade.

A result of this assumption was that all his efforts were centered on football and academics were of little importance to him. He gave minimal effort in the classroom, and his grades reflected this attitude. He reasoned that with his athletic ability, academic requirements would be a nonissue to many college programs which would bend the rules to secure top athletes. This all changed during the summer of his sophomore year when he attended a football camp at a major university.

This university, unlike some others that manipulated academic requirements in order to recruit top players, had strict academic standards for admission. Fenton spent the week in awe of the university, the coaching staff, the stadium, the facilities, everything about the experience. By midweek, he had made up his mind that this was where he would spend his college career.

When the week had drawn to a close, the coaching staff had made a decision that they too wanted Fenton to become a part of their program. They recognized his talent, his coachable attitude, and his potential as an NFL player. However, in the course of conversation, Fenton revealed his academic status to the staff, and there was immediate cause for concern. The coaches explained to Fenton that if he continued to falter in the classroom, it would be impossible for him to be accepted to their institution. They promised that if he would raise his average and class ranking and perform well on his SAT exam, there would be a place for him at their university; if not, then he would have to look elsewhere.

Fenton was initially devastated by this news. He had never been faced with rejection of any kind before, and he was at a loss as to what he could do. He wanted so badly to attend this university but was discouraged because of his academic record. The "truth" he had created in his mind was that he was a terrible student, and as a result, he felt powerless to qualify for this incredible university. He was about to surrender his dream when his guidance counselor had a long conversation with him that altered his perception and the course of his life. The counselor explained that there were options for success available to him if he chose to take a different view of the situation. He explained that if Fenton changed his attitude and began to devote more time to academics, pay more focused attention in class, and seek tutors and extra help, then he would create a whole new academic profile. He proposed the idea that Fenton should apply his athletic attitude toward creating a new academic attitude. All he had to do was keep the goal in mind and alter the way he approached his studies. Fenton considered this advice and began a new perception regarding academics. He paid attention in class, studied, worked with tutors, and attended extra help sessions. As his attitude toward academics changed, so did his work ethic, his pattern of thinking, his belief in his academic abilities, and eventually his performance. He began to approach learning with the same enthusiasm with which he approached football. In time, he created a new pattern of thinking, which in turn created a new belief system about grades, which in turn created a new level of performance. The ending to this story is a happy one; Fenton improved his academic performance to the level required by the university and experienced a successful college career. All it took was a simple shift in perspective to set him on his way.

Still another example of how perception shapes performance is illustrated by an athlete with whom I worked. Toby is a talented athlete who plays softball at a highly competitive level. He came to me with a problem he had been experiencing in his ability to hit safely in games. He told me that no matter how hard he hit the ball, it was always right at the fielders, and he was becoming more and more frustrated by his failures. He stated that the fielders seemed to be everywhere, and he just could not get the ball past them. We devised a strategy that shifted his perception; we drew a diagram of the field and placed an X that represented the position of each fielder. We then looked at the holes or spaces between each fielder; we numbered each hole, making the numbers larger than the X's. Toby began to focus his attention more on the holes than the fielders. The result was that his batting average improved remarkably as his focus shifted from the obstacle of the fielder to the openings or the holes between them.

Perception is also a valuable tool to be used by those looking to lose weight or quit smoking. The people who focus solely upon what they have to give up rather than what they have to gain will invariably return to those unwanted habits of overeating and smoking. Those who succeed in overcoming the challenge of weight loss and becoming smoke free are those individuals who focus on the result of what they will gain rather than what is being left behind. Telling themselves that eating foods that support their goal of a healthier and more appealing body makes the foods that are a part of their new pattern of eating more desirable; this shifts their focus away from thinking of all the foods they can no longer eat. As they focus on their healthy and improved body, those old demons of fattening foods lose their grip on the mind. In time, those same old foods that once were so compelling will become repulsive. That aroma that was once so attractive will make them feel ill at ease.

The same is true of the people who succeed in becoming smoke free. If they shift their focus from no longer being able to smoke to the health benefits of being smoke free, the old demons that once held them captive will eventually slip away. Over time, that alluring smell of a cigarette that causes a craving will be replaced by the sensation of repulsion whenever that odor is present. A waft of an odor that was once so appealing will become repellent. The same smell will render an entirely different sensation. A shift in perception from what one has to lose to what one has to gain is a powerful way to establish new patterns of thought and performance in one's life. It basically comes down to the way you choose to look at things. I heard Dr. Wayne Dyer once say something that resonated so deeply within me: "When you change the way you look at things, the things you look at will change."

To recapitulate, a powerful tool of transformation is to understand perception. By changing the way we view circumstances, we change the pattern of our thinking and ultimately change the outcomes of our life.

<u>Mental Exercise</u>:

- Create columns A and B.

- Think of an unwanted behavior you wish to transform.

- In column A, list all you have to give up.

- In column B, list all you have to gain.

- Cross out or delete all items in column A.

- Place your focus and awareness on what remains in column B.

<u>Your Mental Exercise(s)</u>:

Five

If we think we can...we might.
If we think we can't...we still might.
If we believe we can't...we won't.
If we believe we can...we will.

Tool #2 Certainty

The nature of our mind is that we feel a deep need to be certain—certain that we can, certain that we can't, or certain that we might. Our filtering system is always busy evaluating stimuli and searching the stored files of our subconscious mind to find a response that will relate them in some way to our established belief system and keep us in our comfort zone. If none can be found, then our mind will no longer entertain the stimuli and simply move on to new thoughts.

The tool of certainty is a powerful component in creating the habit of consciously choosing your thoughts.

Consider that you might wish to make a transformation in your body. You really want to shed a few pounds, but all those delicious, fattening foods just don't seem to want to leave your life; your active belief is that you just cannot resist them. You have tried dozens of diets, listened to countless CDs, watched numerous DVDs, and successfully lost those dreaded pounds only to have them return to your body over the course of time. Those old fattening, mouthwatering foods just won't leave you alone. Little by little, you moved back into their clutches, and one day, those new clothes you bought for your slimmer body no longer fit. You become disenchanted with your efforts to transform your body into that beautiful shape you so desired and give up the fight. You know you can never maintain that regimen, so why fool yourself into thinking that you should even continue to try?

Responding this way is living your life by default. Living by default means that you have no control over your response to stimuli. You simply respond according to what is familiar to you because it is "just the way you think." You can conceptualize this by picturing yourself as action oriented versus reaction oriented. Do you want to take control of your life and make decisions based on what you want (action oriented), or do you want to simply react to events in your environment (reaction oriented)? You can choose to switch your orientation, but it takes a decisive mental shift to do this. Once you arrive at the understanding that thoughts are active choices and apply this mode of thinking toward stimuli, then life becomes an experience of creating by design rather than by default. When you learn to choose your thoughts actively, you become responsible for your outcomes rather than allow outcomes to be "just the way it is."

How can the tool of certainty contribute to the process of creating your life by design? Quite simply, by showing you *how* to choose your thoughts.

The first step to creating certainty is to create uncertainty. Since our mind needs to be certain, or sure, creating uncertainty will cause the mind to find a way to become certain. We create uncertainty by simply asking ourselves a question about an issue. Our mind will then search for certainty and receive an answer. Once the answer is defined, then the third stage of the process occurs; we take responsibility and make a conscious choice. We then enter the final stage, which is empowerment.

Let's summarize the process of creating certainty:

- Create uncertainty   (ask a question)

- Create certainty   (Get an answer)

- Take responsibility   (Make a choice)

- Become empowered…

Consider this example of how certainty works. Jake is interested in strengthening his body and decides to join a gym. Although he feels awkward in the beginning, he spends three weeks faithfully going to the gym and is beginning to feel a bit better by doing so. However, somewhere during the fourth week, his positive motivation begins to wane. That old, comfortable belief system that is so deeply rooted in his subconscious mind starts to send him messages. "Jake, come on, you've tried this stuff for a while, just bail out. This is too much work. It's not for you; you'll never keep this up in the long run. Your body is sore, and it takes too much time. Come on, Jake, you don't need to go to the gym today."

Jake is suddenly caught in a moment of doubt and indecision. Part of him believes that old, comfortable voice, but part of him wants to keep going. He is being pulled in two different directions and wants to move forward, but it seems so difficult. What can he do?

The first thing Jake can do is shift his perspective to looking at where he wants to go, not at what he is trying to escape. The best way to evaluate whether a thought is worth changing is to ask yourself, "How is it helpful to me to _____?" If your answer is, "It's not," then that's your cue to change your thinking. For example, Jake can ask himself, "How is it helpful to me to skip the gym?" In this scenario, Jake's answer is, "It's not," signaling him that it is time to evaluate and change his thinking. If the answer is, "It is helpful to me," then Jake can feel confident that he is doing the right thing. By creating a strong picture in his mind of the "new" Jake, he will be telling his subconscious mind to move forward in his pursuit of transformation. The next thing Jake can do is create a dialogue within his mind, using uncertainty, certainty, choice, and empowerment.

"Is going to the gym difficult for me?" (Uncertainty)
"Yes, it is." (Certainty)
"Do I really want to change my body?" (Uncertainty)
"Yes, I do." (Certainty)
"Will it help my goal of getting in shape to skip the gym?" (Uncertainty)
"No." (Certainty)

"Will I feel comfortable with myself if I skip?" (Uncertainty)

"No, I'll feel disappointed later on." (Certainty)

"Then I'll just go, and I'll feel a whole lot better once I've completed my workout." (Choice)

Jake goes to the gym and continues moving toward his goal. (Empowerment)

Whether Jake decides to quit or continue going to the gym is no longer a matter of the old, comfortable way he had conditioned his mind to think; it is now a matter of *choice*. Old habits and patterns of thought are not in control because he has become aware of them. Whatever he chooses to do is now the result of making an active choice, not merely yielding to the old pattern of thinking that it's just the way it is. He has become consciously aware that he is responsible for his actions through the choices he makes in his thought patterns. He has become empowered to create the outcome of his body being in shape by design rather than falling into the old patterns of default.

Certainty is a powerful tool that helps us communicate with our subconscious mind and offers it a new pathway for our thoughts to travel. When we use it with the understanding that it is effective in creating a new program of beliefs in our subconscious mind that will result in a new response to stimuli, we become empowered with the ability to actively choose our thoughts. Knowing that thoughts are always choices and understanding how to consciously choose thoughts is a key component in creating desired outcomes in our lives.

<u>Mental Exercise:</u>

Consider a situation in your life that you are attempting to transform. Be sure to begin by shifting your perception to what you wish to gain rather than dwelling on what you have to give up. Next, create a scenario in your mind that will empower you to remain aligned with your new perception when your old habit of thinking begins to try to have you return to your former comfort zone, telling you that you cannot continue on your course because your new way of thinking and performing is "just too difficult to continue." Construct a dialogue consisting of uncertainty (questions), certainty (answers), and choice (new outcomes). See yourself making the empowering choice. Read your dialogue over several times until you are convinced that you will move forward in the direction that makes you stronger.

<u>Your Mental Exercise(s):</u>

Six

Your mind is always talking. Teaching your mind to speak in a positive way will instruct it to create positive results...Think about that!

Tool #3 Self-Talk

Our mind is always speaking to us. How we speak to ourselves has a powerful impact on how we perform. Let's take a moment to revisit the subconscious mind.

The subconscious mind is the storehouse of our belief systems. It instructs us in how to respond to stimuli based upon the patterns we have created through our thoughts. Our subconscious mind is also literal; it does not differentiate between what is real and what is imagined. It is malleable and can be reshaped over time.

Our mind will believe whatever we tell it; be careful about what you have to say!

Moving forward with the concept of our literal subconscious mind, let us consider the power of self-talk. If we constantly tell our mind that we are inferior, that we can never do certain things, that we are not capable of performing as well as others, we are instructing our subconscious mind to make sure that these outcomes become manifested. Being literal, our subconscious mind will do whatever we tell it to do.

Are you familiar with the story of Aladdin and the magic lamp? When Aladdin rubbed the lamp, a genie would appear and say, "Your wish is my command." Our subconscious mind is akin to that magical genie. It will create for us whatever we command it to. That is why it is very important to speak to it in a positive and present way.

We create a definite vocabulary when speaking to our mind. If our vocabulary is filled with phrases like *I'll never be able to...*; *I always have bad luck*; *I know I'm not good enough*, then our subconscious mind will hold us to these beliefs. Even when we feel inspired to make changes, we will eventually sabotage ourselves and return to our pattern of failure. Why? It is because we have been telling our subconscious mind to do so.

If you find yourself making negative statements that you have deemed unhelpful (for example, how is it helpful for me to focus on my bad luck? It is not helpful.), try to become a detective and look for evidence for and against your thought.

You want to evaluate how accurate the thought is. If you think that you *always* have bad luck, you are probably engaging in a confirmatory bias, where you acknowledge the evidence that supports your thought but disregard evidence that disputes it. You may have bad luck *sometimes*, but doesn't everybody? If you choose to acknowledge the evidence against your thought, you will probably be able to list many times that you didn't have bad luck, therefore disputing your original thought. Think about this: why would you choose to focus on evidence that makes you feel bad when you can choose to focus on evidence that motivates you in a positive way and makes you feel good?

We often unwittingly sabotage our efforts to make effective change by speaking to our mind in the future tense. Phrases like *Someday, I hope to, In the future*, and *I'm trying*, will produce the same limiting effect as phrases of negativity. Why is this so? It is because speaking to our subconscious mind in the future tense is telling it that we do not yet possess whatever it is we are attempting to accomplish. Telling your mind, "I want to lose weight; I'm trying to get in shape," has an entirely different resonance than, "I'm losing weight now; I'm getting my body in shape." Although the difference in wording is subtle, the implication is powerful. This simple rephrasing of a statement that implies transformation in the present rather than the future will instruct the subconscious mind to keep us on the course we've designated. Our goals are no longer separate from us; rather, they become an active part of us. The difference might appear small, but in truth, it is quite significant.

Fake It Till You Make It!

When we understand that our subconscious mind is the storehouse of our beliefs, that it is malleable and can be reprogrammed, we become empowered to consciously transform our belief system from limited to limitless. A powerful way to work on changing our thoughts and actions is to create cognitive dissonance, or an incompatibility between our thoughts and our actions. We don't want to appear like liars, even to ourselves. If we verbally express that we are one way but act a different way, our brains are uncomfortable and want to create consistency between our words and our actions. For example, you want to appear dynamic so you tell a new friend whom you wish to impress that you are an outgoing and friendly person, even though this is not entirely true. You go with your friend to a party where you don't know the other guests. You are surrounded by unfamiliar faces, and your instinct is to be quiet. However, you already verbalized to your friend that you are friendly and outgoing. If you act any other way, you will look inconsistent, like you are a liar. Instead, your brain tells you to act outgoing and friendly because you have already told your friend that those characteristics are part of your personality. When you pretend that you possess whatever personality characteristics or thoughts you *want* to possess, your brain will follow through and pretend you really are that way, just to be consistent. In other words, "Fake it till you make it."

Words are very powerful; use them to generate good feelings.

<u>Vocabulary 101—Connotation:</u>

Words often have either a negative or positive connotation, which in turn creates a feeling we get in our body. Being told, "You are not very smart; you will never learn!" will make us feel differently than being told, "I can see you're having difficulty understanding, but I know you'll be able to understand if you just keep trying. I know you can do it." Things said to us by others are often capable of affecting us for a very long time.

Even more powerful than the words of others are the words we speak to ourselves. We can speak to ourselves as either a coach or a critic; we are free in all moments to speak to ourselves in any manner that we choose. This is why developing a self-talk vocabulary has a most significant correlation in molding our belief systems. The more positive connotations we create in our self-talk, the more successful we will be in creating positive belief systems. Here are a few examples of how negative connotations can be converted into positive connotations:

<u>Negative</u>		<u>Positive</u>
Problem	=	Challenge
Terrible	=	Needs to improve
Change	=	Transformation
Wall	=	Hurdle
Should	=	I will
I'm trying	=	I'm doing
I want to be	=	I am

These are examples of what scientists label neurolinguistic programming, or NLP. Their concept is that thoughts travel along pathways we have created in our mind and produce patented responses to stimuli in a consistent manner. They also theorize that new pathways of thought can be created to produce an entirely different response to the same stimuli. This is referred to as Neuroplasticity. One powerful method of this transformation is to change the way we speak to our mind. Shifting our perspective from the negative to the positive produces new "roads" for our thoughts to travel. As our literal subconscious mind becomes accustomed to the new vocabulary we have developed, it begins to form new perceptions of "I can" rather than "I can't." Once this new vocabulary becomes embedded in our subconscious mind as a belief and then a truth, a new response to stimuli takes place; new expectations become formulated, and a new level of performance becomes possible. A wise exercise to practice is to examine your self-talk vocabulary. Make a list of phrases you constantly speak to your mind. Keep the positive statements intact and alter the statements that are limiting and negative. You will notice over time that the more positive your vocabulary becomes, the more positive outcomes you will experience in your life.

Another tactic to employ is to try to avoid using the words *always* and *never*, as they are very definitive terms. These words are at the end of a spectrum, and using them ignores their polar counterpart and, more important, the gray area in the middle. Saying, "I always fail," or, "I will never finish," means you are catastrophizing, or making things worse than they really are. It is helpful to set up the absolute best and the absolute worst thing that will happen and then acknowledge that neither one is likely to happen. This gray area is usually where the truth lies. Set up the absolute best thought and the absolute worst thought for yourself and then picture them on a spectrum like the one below. After setting up the best and the worst, figure out what lies in the middle; this is probably where your truth lies.

For example, imagine you are nervous about an upcoming interview. What is the absolute worst thing that can happen on the interview? What is the absolute best thing? Is either one likely to happen? Probably not, so let's look at the gray area in the middle.

Worst Case	Gray Area	Best Case
You will not be able to answer any questions and will make a fool of yourself.	You will do a good job at fielding the interviewer's questions.	You will ace the interview and get offered a better position than the one you interviewed for.

You can speak to your mind as either a coach or critic; the choice is always yours.

Snap that Rubber Band—A Simple Way to Convert Negative Self-Talk into Positive:

Moving forward with the understanding of the role that negative self-talk plays in your desire to succeed, here is a simple yet powerful tool that works very well in eliminating that harmful chatter taking place in your mind. Place a rubber band on your wrist. Pay attention to your inner dialogue. Each time you hear yourself speaking to your mind in a negative or limiting way, stretch that rubber band and let it go, and then say, "Stop that! I no longer speak to my mind in that way!" The pain you have inflicted upon your wrist is tantamount to the pain you have inflicted upon your subconscious mind. The rubber band will remind you not to speak to yourself in a negative way. Speaking to your mind in a negative, limiting, and disrespectful way is just as painful to your psyche as snapping the rubber band is to your body. Let us take a moment to understand why this is so.

Our thoughts are constantly instructing our brain to release chemicals and hormones into our body; it is the way the human brain is wired. When we think thoughts of fear, anxiety, and hopelessness, we are telling our brains to release the hormone cortisol into our body. Cortisol is a hormone that creates a feeling of stress within us and ultimately is harmful to our health. The more we entertain such thoughts, the more of this hormone we instruct our brain to release into our body. The more we do so, the more we are held captive by these negative, debilitating thoughts. A cycle of negative thinking and feeling has been set in motion. Conversely, when we think thoughts that are positive and uplifting, we instruct our brain to release other hormones, such as endorphins, into our body, which make us feel good. The better we feel, the more positive thoughts will take place in our mind, thus creating a cycle of positivity. By understanding the power of thought and the influence it has on our body, we learn it is vital to monitor the streams of thoughts we have in our mind. Being aware of our negative thoughts and transforming them into positive thoughts is a powerful technique to master. Use that rubber band as a reminder that negative self-talk fosters negative thoughts that limit us and ultimately cause us harm. Snap them away. That reaction of "Ouch!" is a less-than-gentle reminder of the power of both negative and positive thinking; self-inflicting pain is such a waste of thinking time that could be better spent in a more positive and productive way.

The more positive self-talk your subconscious mind hears, the more it will believe you and the more positive outcomes it will seek to create in your life…Think about that!

Affirmations:

Affirmations are influential statements that we routinely speak to our mind. They can be either negative or positive. A dialogue of positive affirmations is much more beneficial to one's performance in life than one of negative affirmations. The golfer who needs to improve his short game might say, "I am now an excellent putter. My short game is becoming my strength." The person who constantly procrastinates might repeat over and over again, "I am a person of action. It's easy to get things done." Again, create some cognitive dissonance for yourself, make your brain and body uncomfortable and motivated to change in the positive direction and acquire the positive attributes you've already stated you have.

Positive affirmations are powerful because they help in creating a new system of belief, thus creating a new level of performance. Returning to the concept that we create our outcomes in life as the result of our beliefs, that beliefs are thoughts we think over and over again that are charged with emotion, it becomes clear that affirmations play a powerful role in our development. Yet there is a significant factor to understand regarding affirmations. We can recite phrases over and over again, but they will not affect our belief system until the moment we actually *believe* them to be true. Once our mind *believes* what we tell it, then we will have created an entirely new system of thinking and an entirely new way of performing.

Recall for a moment the function of our filtering system and the image of our "guard" who evaluates whether or not to entertain new concepts in our mind. This guard is not eager to allow new patterns of thought to enter our subconscious mind because change of any kind is uncomfortable and we seek to remain comfortable, even if this keeps us in a limiting pattern of thought and performance. Your guard will repel suggestions that make you uncomfortable. The more you persist in convincing your guard to accept a new pattern of thought, the more you repeat over and over again what you wish to become true, the more you will weaken the guard's resistance to change. It will eventually cry out, "Enough already, I believe you!" Once the subconscious mind accepts your suggestion, a new belief system begins to be formed.

Affirmations must be repeated over and over again until they become a type of mantra that you speak to your mind. A method of enhancing their power is to write them down and view them often. Our mind works in pictures, and the more vivid the picture becomes in our mind, the more believable it becomes to us. Another point to consider regarding affirmations is that their power lies in statements that imply you already possess whatever it is you choose to make a part of your life. Statements such as, "I will become a successful salesperson who earns a healthy income," will not be as effective as, "I am a successful salesperson who is earning a healthy income." Although the difference may appear subtle, in reality, it is very significant. The former implies that you do not yet have it; the latter implies it is a part of your life. Once we convince our mind to believe what we are saying, then it will find ways to create it in our life. Affirmations are very powerful and when used in the proper way will help in shaping a powerful belief system in our mind and positive outcomes in our life.

Points to Ponder Regarding Self-Talk:

- Self-talk takes place in our mind on a constant basis.

- Negative self-talk instructs our subconscious mind to seek negative outcomes.

- Positive self-talk instructs our subconscious mind to seek positive outcomes.

- Snap that rubber band; negative self-talk is just as hurtful as physical pain.

- Speak to your mind in a present and positive way.

- Develop powerful affirmations; the moment you believe what you tell your mind is the moment that true transformation takes place in your life.

- Replace limiting phrases with phrases of possibility and empowerment.

<u>Mental Exercise:</u>

Keep a log of the words and phrases you speak most often, both when speaking aloud and when you are speaking to yourself in your mind. For each word and phrase that implies limitations and lack of self-worth, create an alternative word or phrase that implies success and a feeling of value. Refer to your log often and cross out the limiting words and phrases as they become permanently deleted from your self-talk vocabulary.

<u>Your Mental Exercise(s):</u>

Seven

What you allow your mind to think determines how you feel...
simple stuff!

Tool #4 Mindfulness

Mindfulness is simply an awareness of how the thoughts one thinks makes one feel. When people attune themselves to their feelings and become skillful in choosing thoughts that create positive feelings, they will generate thoughts that increase the probability of creating positive outcomes. Understanding that both good and bad feelings are the result of the thoughts we entertain in our mind makes knowing how to actively choose our thoughts a most powerful skill to master. This is why those who learn to consistently choose positive and empowering thoughts will create a happier journey of life than those who allow their minds to think in a random and disordered fashion.

Most people believe that our emotions come before our thoughts, but it actually happens the other way around. Your emotion is your signal that some thoughts were occurring. When you notice your emotion changing, whether you become angry, disappointed, happy, etc., stop and try to decipher what you were just thinking about. For example, a woman is out to lunch with her mother. When the woman places her order for a cheeseburger, she sees her mother raise her eyebrow. The woman becomes angry and hurt and allows one raise of the eyebrow to ruin the rest of the meal. If the woman were able to recognize her change in emotion and take stock of her thoughts, she might be able to assess the accuracy of those thoughts and calm herself down. She may be thinking, *My mother always criticizes me. I can never be like her; my mother thinks I'm fat.*

First, notice that the woman used the words *always* and *never*, which can be our first indicator that the thought is probably not entirely accurate. Her mother may sometimes criticize but probably says things that are complimentary and comforting as well. Maybe the mother is thinner than the daughter. If the daughter exercised some more, she might be able to be thin like her mother. However, the woman needs to stop and assess, "Do I want to be like my mother?" If the answer is "no," then she should choose to let the anger go. If the answer is "yes," then she should funnel the emotion into something positive, such as energy to exercise. Last, the woman needs to ask herself where her evidence is that her mother thinks she is fat. She may have some evidence for this thought, but she may have lots of evidence against it, as well. *My mother sometimes comments on what I eat, but she usually tells me I'm beautiful and that I look great, so maybe my thought is not entirely accurate.*

It is extremely helpful to write down your negative thoughts as they come to you. After each thought ask yourself, "What else?" to make sure you are getting all of your thoughts out. You may be surprised by all the negativity going on in your mind. Sometimes seeing your negative thoughts on paper can help you to realize how detrimental your thinking can be to your emotions and level of confidence.

Our brain is a powerful organ that responds to the instructions we create within it. A simple analogy would be to think of the brain as a computer processor. It will perform its operations based upon whatever data has been programmed into it. The processor simply evaluates the data and responds accordingly. Our brain functions in a similar fashion. We have programmed data into our subconscious mind based on our beliefs. Whenever a stimulus is presented, our subconscious mind produces a response that is familiar to us. If the stimulus is one that causes us to think thoughts that create tension and anxiety, then we are instructing our brain to produce chemicals and hormones that make us feel discomfort. When we feel a constant discomfort or unease within our bodies, we become more vulnerable to illness and the breakdown of healthy cells. Conversely, when a stimulus causes us to generate positive and uplifting thoughts, we then instruct our brain to produce chemicals and hormones that create ease and comfort within our bodies. These chemicals and hormones serve to strengthen our immune system and keep harmful cells from developing into illness.

When we come to understand both the power that our thoughts have to maintain our well-being and their potential to create breakdowns in our bodies and that thoughts can be actively controlled, then we become empowered to create a happier and healthier life. Even if we have arrived at a moment in time where our bodies have already become afflicted by disease, we can still create a happier and more fulfilling journey through the ability to choose our thoughts and create positive outcomes.

A simple shift in thinking can create a powerful shift in our living...Think about that!

<u>Transition Thoughts—The Key to
Choosing Positive Thoughts:</u>

Transition thoughts are thoughts that move us from a negative, debilitating state of mind to one that is positive and uplifting. The prefix *trans* means to move across (e.g., transportation, transmit, transgress). The more one practices creating transition thoughts, the more quickly one can replace a moment of anxiety with a moment of peace.

Let us consider a situation that can typically evoke high anxiety for many. You have an important appointment and leave your home a bit later than you expected. Within minutes, you find yourself in the midst of a huge traffic jam. You tune your radio to the local traffic station and discover an accident has occurred further along your route. There are no alternative routes available, so you will have to work your way through the bumper-to-bumper traffic. You realize that you will be at least twenty minutes late for your important appointment. How you spend the next twenty minutes will be entirely up to you. You can curse, scream, and become agitated and angry. You can spend the worst twenty minutes of your life filled with tension while moving toward your destination. Ask yourself, "How would it be helpful to me to curse, scream, and become agitated and angry?" The answer is, "It would not," since doing so will not get you to your destination any faster and will only serve to make you miserable. You do have other options available to you as well. You can use the time to listen to music, a talk show, or a book on tape. If you have a hands-free cell phone, you can call a friend to help you calm down. You can create daydreams or creative ideas about a project you wish to work on. The options are endless. In other words, the wiser choice is not to stress about the things you can't change and control; choose to focus on the things that you can.

You might spend the first five minutes feeling miserable before you begin to shift your thoughts toward those that will make you feel more at ease. This would result in five minutes of frustration and fifteen minutes of relaxation. The fact of the matter is that you have a *choice* as to how you will respond, and the choice you make will affect how you feel. Your decision as to which thoughts to choose will affect how you spend those twenty minutes. It is the same amount of time, but you are empowered to choose different ways of spending it; it is always your choice.

Another example of transition thoughts would be for the person who is scheduled to speak publicly and whose mind is filled with anxiety and fear. If this person focuses only on his or her fear, then he or she is likely to falter in the speaking engagement. However, the feeling of being ill at ease can be replaced by the feeling of being at ease by creating transition thoughts. Here is an example of how this might be done:

- *I despise public speaking; I know I'll make a fool of myself.* (Where is your evidence for that thought? Is there an alternative way to see the situation?)

- *I'm too nervous to concentrate; I'll never remember what I want to say.* (Refrain from using the word *never*; it makes the situation very black and white with no grey area in the middle.)

- *However, I have spoken before the public before and did very well.* (Use your evidence of past successes.)

  o *I'm usually comfortable once I get going.*

  o *I've received many compliments about the job I do.*

  o *I really know what I'm talking about.*

  o *I know my speaking will help people.*

- *Hey, I can do this.* (Change the thought!)

- *Let's get it going!*

Below is another example of how creating transition thoughts can move one from the negative to the positive. Consider the inner dialogue of someone who is in the process of creating a healthier body but is struggling with the stimulus of food that is counterproductive to the goal of maintaining a healthy eating regimen.

<u>Create Transition Thoughts</u>

I can't stand this diet! I want to eat.
I did lose a few pounds though.
I'm beginning to understand healthy eating choices.
A few people told me I'm looking pretty good.
I'm getting control of my body.
Hey, I don't really need that food!

By learning to pay attention to your feelings, you become empowered to change your mood from negative to positive. Feeling good is a much better way to spend time than feeling bad. A simple transition to your pattern of thinking will set you on your way…if you choose for it to be so.

Mental Exercise:

Moving from "I can't" toward "I can"

Think of the "I can'ts" that are a predominant part of the thought processes that are preventing you from moving forward toward some goals that you wish to accomplish. Imagine yourself on a moving walkway that is powered by your thoughts. Positive thoughts set it in motion and negative thoughts cause it to stall. Begin at point A, which is the point of "I can't." At the opposite end of this moving walkway is the point of "I can." Set this walkway in motion by writing down transition thoughts that will move you toward point B, the point of "I can."

This is a very powerful exercise for it conditions your mind to move forward by actively seeking possibilities rather than remaining stagnant because of excuses that keep you locked in your comfort zone.

Your Mental Exercise(s):

ANTs

There are many varieties of ants that inhabit our earth, and they are valuable insects in our web of life. However, if you awoke one day to find your home filled with a swarm of ants, they would suddenly become unwanted invaders. What would you do about these intruders? You would likely search for an effective way to rid your home of these uninvited pests. Having ants in the home is an unpleasant experience for most of us.

There is another type of "ant" that produces a feeling of discomfort within us. The place where these ANTs reside is in the mind. The type of ANT that exists in one's mind is an automatic negative thought.

ANTs keep us limited and often inhibit us from stepping beyond the comfort zone of our beliefs to try something new and challenging. They keep us safe and secure, even if this safety produces feelings of anxiety, fear, and inferiority.

The athlete who tells himself he can never make the game-winning play, the student who tells herself she can never score 100 percent on a test, the salesman who tells himself he is not capable of closing that great deal, and the author who is convinced that no publisher will seriously consider her work are all expressing the ANTs that live in their minds. Their response to those stimuli is an automatic "I can't." These ANTs have been allowed to infest their minds through the thoughts they have entertained over a long period of time and have become their truths, even if these truths are not entirely true.

Is it possible to "exterminate" these unwanted pests? The answer is a definite "Yes!"

An effective method of "exterminating" ANTs from your mind starts with paying attention to them. Take the time to notice your response to stimuli that threaten to take you beyond your comfort zone. If there are things you would really like to do or try but automatically respond with "I can't," take a few moments to understand that your response is the result of the thoughts you have created as your truth and know that a change in your pattern of thinking will produce a change in the way you respond. Keep in mind that the process of extermination is likely to take some time to become effective; however, focusing on the elimination of these pests will keep you focused upon succeeding. It is important to keep this statement in mind: *by focusing more on where you want to go, you will focus less on what you are afraid to leave.*

My friend Bill told me a story of how eliminating a cluster of ANTs from his mind changed his life in a powerful way.

Bill had been working as a manager in a large utility company and was doing very well. A higher-paying position as a contract negotiator became available, and his friends encouraged him to apply for the position. Bill's initial response was, "I could never do that!" and he declined to file an application. However, as his friends continued to speak to him about how great he would be in that role, Bill's mind began a gradual shift from focusing on all the reasons he "could never succeed" to entertaining thoughts of *I might be able to do this.* Little by little, his mind began the gradual transition of moving beyond the limiting thoughts that kept him in his comfort zone to the limitless thoughts of possibility. When he finally arrived at the moment where his *thought* of "I can't" was replaced with the *belief* of "I can," he submitted an application for the job.

The end result is obvious; Bill was finally interviewed for the position and was accepted. He eliminated the ANTs that told him he could never succeed in the role and went on to have a very successful and fulfilling career as a contract negotiator. By changing his pattern of thinking, he changed both his professional and personal life.

All it took for Bill to change the circumstances of his life was to change the thoughts he entertained in his mind. What worked for Bill can work for us all. We can change our response to any stimulus by changing the patterns of thought in our mind and in doing so can change the pattern of how we live our lives.

Mental Exercise:

Exterminating ANTs from your mind:

Keep a log of the ANTs that are a regular part of your thinking process. Note the stimulus for each ANT and your exact response. Next, select a single ANT and devise a plan to exterminate it from your thought process. When the ANT is exterminated, return to your list and select another ANT to eliminate. Continue this process until you have successfully freed your mind of these unwanted pests.

Your Mental Exercise(s):

Eight

If you can really see it, you can really be it; it really does work that way!

Tool #5 Visualization

Visualization is a powerful tool that has been employed by successful people throughout all ages in time. Simply stated, visualization is the ability to foresee your desired future and draw it toward you. There is nothing mystical about visualization, although its power often renders one mystified. Like all skills acquired in life, visualization is a process that once mastered produces powerful outcomes.

Visualization has long been practiced in the athletic arena. Successful athletes are known to spend many hours before a contest picturing their every move as well as imagining their response to every situation, both positive and negative. The more one prepares one's mind for the competition, the easier it will be for one to respond in a positive fashion from a position of strength. Gary Mack, in his book *The Mind Gym*, tells this story of Nolan Ryan, the great Hall of Fame pitcher:

> The marquee athlete uses the mind to program the body. Listen to Nolan Ryan, the Hall of Fame pitcher, describe his routine: "The night before a game I lie down, close my eyes, relax my mind and body, and prepare myself for the game. I go through the entire lineup of the other team, one batter at a time. I visualize exactly how I am going to pitch to each hitter, and I see and feel myself throwing exactly the pitches that I want to throw. Before I ever begin to warm up at the ballpark, I've faced all of the opposition's hitters four times, and I've gotten my body ready for exactly what it is I want to do."[1]

Visualization is far from limited to athletes. I once had a surgeon tell me how he employs visualization before performing surgery on his patients:

> The night before a surgery, I sit quietly and perform the entire procedure in my mind. I see the patient, the surgical staff, the OR, all the instruments and monitors. I see myself from the moment I enter the OR until the moment I leave it. I pay attention to every detail of the surgery, from beginning to end. By the morning of the surgery, I've successfully completed the entire operation in my mind.

Why is visualization so powerful? To understand why it is so effective, we must first consider how it works.

---

1. Gary Mack, David Casstevems, *Mind Gym, An Athlete's Guide to Inner Excellence* (New York: McGraw-Hill, 2001), p 158.

We should understand that our mind works in pictures. For some, these pictures are in the form of feeling (tactile) or in the form of hearing (auditory). For others, it is a clear picture in the mind (visual). However, it is important for an individual to know that for all stimuli, there is a response that creates a vision of some kind. For example, look at each of the following words and pay attention to what forms in your mind:

- Car

- Theater

- Park

- Mother / Father

- Teacher

- Beautiful

For each example above, the stimulus presented to your mind formed an impression; your mind instantly created a picture of some kind. Understanding that your mind works in pictures is the first step toward honing your visualization skills. The second step toward employing your visualization skills is to revisit the subconscious mind.

The working of our subconscious mind is instrumental in influencing our beliefs. To review, the subconscious mind is where all of our experiences and beliefs exist. It is important to remember that it is both literal and malleable. By using the proper mental tools, we can effectively instruct our subconscious mind to bring forth to our lives whatever we tell it to. The moment we transform our thought pattern from *thinking* to *believing*, we become empowered to transform a vision into a reality.

Keep your eye on the prize; it makes the effort so much easier.

Many people have heard of visualization and have tried using it in a cursory type of way only to abandon their efforts because they found it just did not work for them. Like any tool, one must use it often to get a true understanding and feel for how it will serve one best. Purchasing a computer and learning only one function does not make the computer a limited tool; the limitation is in the mind of the user who does not make himself or herself aware of the computer's capabilities. If he or she will take the time to delve more deeply into the computer's functions and capabilities, the computer will become a valued and powerful tool. The same is true of the power of visualization.

What more is there to understand about visualization than simply creating a vivid picture in the mind? To begin, keep in mind the way that you are capable of influencing the subconscious mind. Next, understand the significance of sensory input. Our mind works on a stimulus-response basis. The more emotion that is attached to the stimulus, the stronger the response becomes. It is important to add to your vision the elements of your five senses. Make your vision as rich and detailed as you possibly can.

- Where are you?

- What do you look like, sound like?

- Are there others around you? If so, what are they doing, saying, and wearing?

- Next, pay close attention to what you are feeling.

- Which emotions are you experiencing?

- Study your body language; what does it project?

- Which sounds do you hear? Which aromas do you smell?

If there are tastes involved and sensory stimulation attached to your vision, allow your imagination to experience them. Remember, your subconscious mind does not distinguish between things real and imagined, so use this to your advantage.

Another important point to consider regarding visualization is to begin at the end and work in reverse. What this means is that whatever outcome you wish to accomplish, create a vivid vision with sensory input attached of what things will look like when you have *completed* whatever you have visualized. How will you appear, and how will you feel once your vision has been made manifest? What does your body language project? Who will be there? What will you be wearing? Where will you be? Keep this picture of completion strong and vivid in your mind, and then retrace your journey in your mind until you reach the point where you are in the present moment. Remember, begin with the ending and end at the beginning. In visualizing this way, you will actually be drawing the result toward you. The more you experience something in your imagination, the more your subconscious mind will believe that it is real. The stronger the belief that you create in your mind, the more certain the desired outcome will be made manifest in your life.

Nat, an acquaintance of mine, told me the story of how he used visualization from end point to starting point. Nat was informed that he had cancer and had to undergo an extensive surgery that would attempt to successfully remove a malignant tumor. Nat understood the power of visualization and the power of his mind. For two weeks prior to his surgery, he parked his car across the street from the exit of the hospital and "saw" himself walking out of the hospital smiling and in total health, with his family escorting him. In his mind, he "saw" the happy procession, the celebration of his successful surgery, taking place. As he convalesced in the hospital, he kept this image strong and clear in his mind. Nat smiled when he told me that the picture he had created in his mind was *exactly* what took place upon his release from the hospital.

The more we focus on what we lack, the less our chances of making our visions become reality. Don't focus so much on how; focus on what you truly want.

The Vision Buster: Focusing Too Much on "How"

Another point to consider about the power of visualization is to understand the greatest vision buster of them all, which is the simple question, "How?" We very often become absorbed in dreams and visions of things we would love to have become a part of our lives only to have the moment interrupted by the great question of doom, "How in the world can

I do this?" As soon as we interrupt our vision with "How?" a series of reasons (which are likely excuses our minds create to keep us in our comfort zone) begin to dominate our thinking. Thoughts like *I don't have the time, I don't have the money, I'm not skilled enough, There are no opportunities*, etc., are the greatest saboteurs of dreams and visions. When one learns to truly master the power of visualization, one arrives at the realization that rather than focusing on how to make one's vision become manifest, the real "secret" is to know that the "how" will happen. How is this possible? It returns to the key element of belief. If we *think* we can, we might; if we *believe* we can, we will.

Returning once more to the power of our subconscious mind, we can form a clearer understanding of how this concept works. When we program or reprogram our subconscious mind to seek possibilities rather than limitations, our awareness shifts from why we *cannot* succeed to finding a way that we *will* succeed. The manifestation of our vision might take longer than we have imagined and might present more challenges than we had anticipated, yet it will become manifest if we persist in our belief that it will. Obstacles will often present themselves and alterations in plans might be necessary, but obstacles can be overcome. The positively motivated person will perceive the obstacle as a hurdle, while the nonbeliever will see it as an insurmountable barrier. A hurdle can be overcome; a barrier is often too difficult to move past. How we proceed in the pursuit of our visions is ultimately the result of our perceptions, which are fueled by our beliefs.

I once worked in a school with a woman whose initial job was that of a hall monitor. She sat at a desk and issued passes to visitors. Her salary was minimal and was not nearly enough to sustain her family's finances. In conversation one day, she revealed that she had always desired to be a teacher but had never completed her education. At thirty-eight years of age, she had three elementary-aged children and a husband who was frequently unemployed. Becoming a teacher at this particular time in life would likely be too difficult because of time commitments and the lack of financial means. We frequently discussed the value of teachers and how great she would be in that role. For a long while, she passed the thought off as an idle daydream until a moment arrived when she could actually "see" herself as a teacher. Her thought of why it would never be possible transformed into how she could actually make it happen. She fully understood the financial, emotional, and physical obstacles that would be in her path but the vision of earning her degree became more powerful than the obstacles that stood before her. She enrolled in one course and placed her feet on the path. For the next several years, she forged ahead one course at a time, always looking forward. She finally made her vision into a reality, received her teaching degree, and secured a teaching position. But her vision became expanded, and she continued her education in administration; she is currently an assistant principal. This woman did not listen to those who told her she was too old to begin a new career, could not afford to do so, and would never have the time or energy to be a mother, wife, and student. What drove her to prove the naysayers wrong? It was her vision that filled her mind with possibilities. She overcame the vision buster of "How?" and maintained her focus on the prize. She used two age-old adages to keep her focused on her success: "Where there's a will, there's a way," and "Nothing is impossible to one who truly believes." She learned to step out of the comfort zone of excuses and into the arena of manifestation.

Reviewing the Principles of Visualization:

- Visualize in real time.

- Make your vision as vivid as you possibly can.

- Attach rich sensory input and emotions to your vision.

- Keep your vision clear and strong in your mind at all times.

- Perceive obstacles as hurdles that can be overcome.

- Believe that you can…and you will!

Mental Exercise:

Create a vision journal. Write down what you really want in your life. Make your journal entry as detailed and vivid as you possibly can. Attach as many sights, sounds, tastes, touches, fragrances, and feelings as you possibly can. Feel free to find pictures of your completed vision and paste them in your journal. Visit your vision journal each day. Enhance and revise it as often as you feel the need to do so.

Your Mental Exercise(s):

Nine

A picture is worth a thousand words...That's why it's so important to make only pictures of success in your mind!

Tool #6 Imagery

Imagery is another powerful tool of the mind that involves creating mental "pictures." Both visualization and imagery stimulate the conscious mind to create images that are believable, and each alerts the subconscious mind to produce familiar responses to stimuli. Each is a valuable tool in programming the subconscious mind to respond in a positive way.

Although similar, visualization and imagery differ as well. Visualization creates precise mental images regarding specific goals and events. The athlete who pictures the arena, the opponent, the situation, and the actual performance is visualizing. The surgeon who performs the entire surgery in his mind prior to the operation, seeing the patient, OR, instruments, and nurses is visualizing as well. The same is true for the student studying for a test who sees herself in the testing room answering questions with a relaxed posture and remaining composed when responding to confusing questions. In each scenario, it holds true that the more sensory input that is attached to the vision, the more likely it becomes that a successful outcome is achieved.

Imagery is also a tool that influences the conscious and subconscious mind to respond to stimuli in a consciously programmed manner. Unlike visualization that creates specific images of specific events, imagery is a mental device that creates more abstract images that influence the mind to respond in a specific way.

An example of imagery is depicted in the image below.

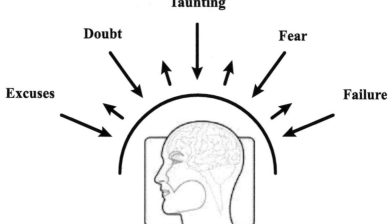

The above illustration was created for G., a talented high school pitcher who frequently had difficulty performing on a consistent basis throughout the game. He would often lose his composure when opponents taunted him and when coaches began shouting at him. He would fall apart and fail to finish the game because he had allowed his mind to be filled with thoughts of fear, doubt, failure, and excuses.

G. learned to create a mental image of a barrier, a mental helmet surrounding his head that deflected negative comments from opponents, coaches, and fans. In his mind, he "saw" all negative comments aimed at him being deflected into the atmosphere. He created a picture of his mind being open to only thoughts of his strength and expertise. G. practiced thinking of this image many times a day until his mind finally believed it was capable of being unaffected by the stimuli that had once unraveled him. The result was a new way of thinking and a new way of performing. At the end of his senior year, G. had been awarded a scholarship to a college that boasts of a very successful baseball program.

An image I use to clear my mind of negative thoughts that begin to dominate my thinking is of a room in my mind that is cluttered with cobwebs and dust, which represent negativity. I envision myself with a broom sweeping away the cobwebs and using a vacuum to eliminate the dust. I then "see" my mind as a clear and orderly room that I begin to paint with clean, bright colors created by positive and powerful thoughts that are streaming through large, magnificent windows.

Two important concepts to consider are that the mind works in pictures and imagination is the birthplace of creative ideas. All action begins first in the mind. By learning to control our thoughts and consciously creating images of success, we are programming our subconscious mind to respond to stimuli in a way we choose rather than responding in a "just the way I am" manner. In essence, we are then creating life by design rather than default.

Learning to use imagery effectively, like each of the mental tools described within this book, takes time and practice. Like all habits we have developed in our life, it requires patience, persistence, and perseverance. Creating a new positive habit is more difficult than defaulting to an old negative habit, but the end result is worth the time and attention you will invest in the process. A bad habit is easy to form but creates negativity; a good habit is difficult to form but creates positive outcomes in life. You are free to create any habit that you choose.

Our mind works in pictures. Create pictures of yourself succeeding…It works!

The image below is one that I often use with clients to illustrate the power of choosing one's thoughts.

Think of your brain as a machine. When you think a positive thought, you press a button that releases hormones that make you happy, light, and free.

When you think negative thoughts, you consequently press a button that makes you feel upset and stressed.

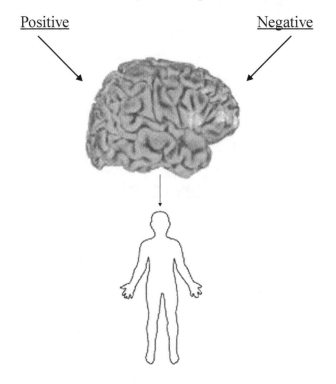

Positive   Negative

This image is used to remind you that how you feel is directly proportionate to how you think. If you perceive your brain as a machine that manufactures chemicals in your body based upon the thoughts you think, then you become aware that negative and limiting thoughts of fear, worry, anxiety, inferiority, jealousy, and hatred are destructive, not only to your mental well-being, but also to your physical well-being. Focusing regularly on the negative will eventually have an adverse effect on your immune system, while focusing regularly on positive thoughts will have a positive effect. This simple image can be a powerful tool in reminding you to choose positive thoughts that are uplifting and beneficial over thoughts that are negative and destructive. Once you begin to master choosing your thoughts, you begin to master creating outcomes in your life, rather than simply responding to circumstances in a "just the way I am" or "just the way it is" fashion. Like all other acquired skills, the more you practice, the better you become at applying this skill. It is no different from practicing a musical instrument, an athletic skill, or a proven sales technique. One important point to ponder is that for practice to be effective, you must practice with the belief that you are becoming empowered. The age-old adage that practice makes perfect is only a partial truth. The real truth is that perfect practice makes perfect.

Another image I encourage clients to create is that of a garden of fertile soil. Whatever is planted in this soil will grow and flourish. If you plant thorns, then thorns will grow. However, if you plant flowers, then flowers will grow. Think of your mind as a garden of fertile soil. If you sow thoughts of negativity and limitations, thoughts of things always going wrong, then that is what the fertile soil of your mind will reap. However, if you sow thoughts of success and abundance, then success and abundance will grow. The "secrets" of creating images that are effective in producing desired outcomes in life are understanding that you are capable of creating new belief systems in your subconscious mind and having faith that what you create will become manifested in your life. The moment you truly believe it is possible...it is!

Imagination is the key to creation. All actions are preceded by thought. The more active your imagination is in creating images of success and abundance, the more success and abundance will become a part of your belief system and the more success and abundance will appear in your life. Keep in mind that the process takes time to develop and cultivate, but if you persist in practicing positive imagery, then in time, you will master the skill. The moment that mastery arrives is the moment you believe it to be true. When your "guard" finally allows your mind to admit thoughts of success into your subconscious belief system, you then become empowered to create the life you envision in your mind. Imagery is a powerful tool; learn to use it to create your best life possible.

<u>Mental Exercise:</u>

Imagination Time:

Designate anywhere from five to twenty minutes each day as "imagination time."

During this time, allow your mind to form as many images as you possibly can that make you experience positive emotions and feelings. Select images that will make you smile and feel good. Next, make a mental note of your favorite image or images and revisit them periodically throughout the day. Keep this thought in your mind as you play with your images: *Imagination is the seed that makes all realities grow.*

Barrel Exercise:

Create an image of two large barrels. Place a large P, for positive, on one and a large N, for negative, on the other. Spend some time each day paying attention to your active thoughts and imagine them dripping from your mind into the appropriate barrel. Notice which barrel is becoming fuller. If your negative barrel begins to become too full, spend some time emptying these negative and limiting thoughts and begin to focus upon placing more thoughts in your positive barrel.

<u>Your Mental Exercise(s):</u>

Ten

However your body allows you to move…move gracefully.

Tool #7 Energy Management

Most people are interested in living their best life possible. Even for those who have allowed their bodies to become out of shape, for whom finances might be difficult, or who have a heart that may be broken, for example, it is still possible to live your best life possible. Understanding how to manage your thoughts and energy can transform a mind that focuses on limitations to a mind that focuses on possibilities. Your living time can be spent in any number of perceptions. What you believe life to be is exactly what it will be.

If you wish to optimize the power of your mind, it is wise to focus your attention upon your energy. The more energy you put into life, the more energy you will have to take from it. The obvious links to creating a higher energy are in choosing to eat and sleep properly; to refrain from abuses of alcohol, drugs, and tobacco; and to do some form of exercise. There are volumes written about the benefits of developing a healthy regimen for your body. However, it is important to understand that regimens that bring health to your body begin with and are sustained by the health of your mind.

We have discussed how beliefs are formed, how to program your subconscious mind, and how to use the tools of certainty, perception, self-talk, mindfulness, visualization, and imagery. Energy management is yet another important tool that will help you in living your best life possible.

Decisions made through a clear and relaxed mind are the most effective decisions we can make.

Even in our most harried and busy moments, we are still capable of making clear decisions. A relaxed mind is not a lazy mind; a relaxed mind is one that is not overwhelmed with thoughts of fear and anxiety. The more you learn to relax your mind, the more you will be able to make clear and effective decisions.

An old buddy of mine, Johnny Pontiff, once wrote a song entitled, "Speed Yoga." Its lyrics depict someone who is constantly in a hurry to get somewhere that he can never seem to get to and also ironically rushes to get to a state of relaxation. The theme of the song is that some of us push ourselves so hard to try to find the meaning of life that we never actually take the time to discover just what it might really be.

Our pattern of thinking produces physical sensations in our body that either cause us to feel good or to feel bad. A body depleted of energy is often the result of a mind depleted of peaceful patterns of thinking. Endorphins are chemicals released into the body by the brain that make you feel good; they are produced by the positive and uplifting thoughts that you are able to think in your mind. Conversely, cortisol is a chemical released into your body by the brain that makes you feel anxious and depressed; it is the product of the negative thoughts you think in your mind. Knowing this empowers you to use the tool of mindfulness to control what you instruct your brain to release into your body. When you are immersed in thoughts of fear, anxiety, frustration, or feeling sad, understanding that the uneasiness you are experiencing in your body can be changed to ease simply by changing your thoughts empowers you to be able to do so. Once you recognize that your thoughts are depleting your energy, there are numerous ways you can revive your vitality.

Pay attention to your breath. As long as you have breath, you have life. As long as you have life, the potential to live your best life possible exists.

One thing most of us take for granted is our breath. Our breath is the force that sustains the life within us. Controlling our breathing can have a significant impact on our clarity of mind. The more relaxed and clear our mind becomes, the more positive and empowering thoughts have the potential to enter, and the more effective choices we will be empowered to make. Why is this so? How can paying attention to our breathing help us in our thinking? There is a simple physiological answer to this question.

Our bodies require oxygen to sustain life. We inhale oxygen, which purifies our body, and exhale carbon dioxide, which releases toxins. When our breathing is constantly shallow, both the intake of oxygen and the release of carbon dioxide are minimal and the benefits of the breathing process become limited. However, by increasing our intake of oxygen and release of carbon dioxide, we can help the tissues, organs, and systems of our body function more effectively. By breathing deeply, we increase the efficiency of our body and mind.

Since breathing is a part of our autonomic nervous system, most of us really do not pay attention to it. Breathing, like other parts of our autonomic nervous system, takes place naturally and is regulated by our subconscious mind. Our conscious mind has so much to deal with that we simply allow these automatic systems to "do their thing." However, if we increase our awareness of our ability to regulate our body's automatic functions consciously, we become capable of using our mind in a more powerful and efficient way. There are numerous ways to regulate and increase our body's energy systems. I will suggest a few that work very well for me and my clients. If they resonate within you, use them. You might even develop a number of your own techniques to increase your energy level and life force of energy.

The deeper we breathe, the more deeply we relax.

<u>Belly Breathing</u>

A simple technique to increase the depth of your breath is belly breathing. By deepening your intake of oxygen, you are able to relieve stress placed on the tissues, organs, and systems of your body. Here is how it is done:

Place one hand on your stomach and inhale slowly and deeply; allow your breath to sink all the way into your stomach. When your stomach has risen to its full capacity, pause for a moment, then use your hand to push it in gently, and begin the exhalation process. Do this several times until you are consistently able to draw your breath all the way into your stomach.

Once you have mastered getting the breath into your stomach, you can make it go deeper still. As you inhale, place one hand on your chest while the other continues to rest on your stomach. As you inhale, pay attention to the hand on your chest. Try to keep your chest cavity as still as you possibly can. Focus on getting your breath all the way down into your stomach. Focusing on the stillness of your chest will increase your awareness of your breath sinking deeper into your stomach.

Remember, the deeper your intake of oxygen, the greater the release of carbon dioxide from your body on the out breath. This cycle of deep breathing will relax your body and mind, offering you moments of clarity and renewed vitality.

I use belly breathing with athletes throughout the course of a competition. Using this simple breathing technique helps them to remain relaxed in their body and clear in their mind. It is a good idea to practice this breathing exercise several times throughout the day. If you make a conscious effort to do so, you will be taking active control of the physical potential of your body and the mental efficiency of your mind.

Clear the Clutter

Some people are adept at keeping their homes neat and organized. They have a place for everything and keep everything in its proper place. People also exist who live in a constant state of clutter. They have things piled all over the place, stacked under furniture, scattered throughout their living space. Most of these people will straighten things up for a while and vow to keep organized and neat, only to return to the old habits of clutter and disarray.

Living in a cluttered material world can certainly make life difficult, but living in a cluttered mental world makes life more difficult still. A mind that races with anxiety, fear, guilt, worry, deadlines, difficult relationships, and so on is a mind that is depleted of focused energy. When you become depleted of mental energy, this will have an adverse effect on your physical energy as well. Just as we can unclutter our physical environment, we can also unclutter our mental environment. By becoming aware of the piles of thoughts accumulating in our mind, we can take a moment to rearrange our thoughts and put everything in its proper place. Doing so will help to create a focused and clear mind. A clear and focused mind will help you to live your best life possible.

Think of your mind as a computer. When we first purchase our computer, all the programs are organized and running to maximum efficiency, and we can enjoy working with its speed and precision. However, over time, we are apt to download many programs and create numerous files, and if we fail to take the simple and easy steps to keep our data organized, eventually, our computer will operate at a much slower speed, and even "freeze." We are then likely to invest an inordinate amount of time and perhaps a large sum of money trying to get our computer back up to speed. Had we performed our simple maintenance tasks on a regular schedule, we could have saved our valuable time and money and experienced much less anxiety and stress.

Just as there are simple maintenance tasks available for your computer, there are also simple maintenance tasks available for your mind. There are simple steps you can take to keep your mind organized and clear. Investing a minimal amount of time and energy toward this goal is quite beneficial. All it takes is the conscious creation of a simple yet powerful habit. Consider what I do several times each day. You may be inclined to adopt or adapt my method to suit your own taste. Whatever you choose for yourself is appropriate. The goal is simply to unclutter your mind and create a clear and focused pattern of thinking.

I begin by taking deep and relaxing belly breaths and then create an image of a computer screen. Using my imagination, I view numerous programs running simultaneously and data scattered in an intermittent and disorganized manner. In my mind's eye, I take a mental mouse and click on edit. I scroll down to "select all" and click. When all the text on my mental screen becomes highlighted, I press "delete" and watch the entire screen go blank. I stare at the blank screen as long as my concentration allows, which is usually from sixty to ninety seconds. Staring at the blank screen helps me to clear the clutter in my mind and return to active thinking, feeling refreshed and in control of my thought processes. Taking control of my thoughts helps me to take control of my feelings. Feeling positive and uplifted offers me more personal power to accomplish whatever I desire to accomplish than does feeling pressured, stressed, and unhappy.

It is a wise idea to create techniques that help you to clear your mental clutter on a regular basis. It is a simple habit that, once in place, will energize both your body and your mind.

Take a vacation as often as possible, if only in your mind.

Take a Mental Break

We have all experienced stress in our lives. Stress is a natural part of the living condition. We can also understand the negative consequences of a life that is constantly filled with stress. When our mind and body reach the point where we become totally absorbed by stress, we are bound to experience a mental or physical breakdown of some type, perhaps both. Stress can steal our valuable living time, if we allow it to.

Stress in itself is not always a bad thing. Stress is often the catalyst that sets our mind and body in motion toward achieving a goal. When perceived with a positive outlook, stress can become a positive influence. It offers us that push or nudge that we need to get ourselves going. It is not stress itself that creates breakdowns in our mind and body, rather it is how we respond to stress that renders the consequences either positive or negative.

When you find yourself mired in a stressful situation, it is wise to pay attention to what is taking place within you. Sensations such as headaches, the inability to sleep or concentrate, stiffness in your limbs, and tightness in your chest are signals that are being sent to your body that something is about to give. If you fail to listen to these warning signals, you will likely be affected.

We can relieve the impact of constant stress, if we choose to do so. We might not be able to eliminate the people, places, or circumstances that are causing us to be ill at ease; however, we can develop strategies that will allow us to step away from their clutches and refresh our energy and perceptions, and doing so will disempower the negative feelings that are depleting our energy level. We might not be able to alter circumstance, but we can alter our response to circumstance, which will allow us to renew our energy. How can this be done? One way to relieve stress is to simply take time each hour to breathe deeply. The benefits of deep breathing have been discussed earlier in this chapter. There is another highly effective method of stepping out of stress and into moments of relaxation. This method is "going on vacation," if only in your mind.

Vacations are wonderful opportunities to "get away from it all." By placing ourselves in a different environment with varying routines, sights, sounds, and people around us, we are sometimes able to step away from the physical environment in which we feel captured by stress. We are sometimes able to create a "new" environment for ourselves by supplying changeable routines. We might not be able to take a physical vacation whenever we desire; however, we can take a mental vacation whenever we choose to do so. We can experience some degree of relief that will benefit our physical and emotional state of being by stepping away from the situation, if only in our mind.

It is a good idea to slow your pace down from time to time. You can notice more when traveling at twenty miles per hour than you can when traveling at one hundred miles per hour...Think about that!

Cycles of the Brain

Beta 14–21 CPS (cycles per second)
Alpha 7–14 CPS
Theta 4–7 CPS
Delta 0–4 CPS

A deeper understanding of the cycles of the brain will offer you a valuable means of creating a relaxed state of mind. Our brain waves function at four basic cycles. The cycle where our brain is most active is called beta. In this particular cycle, our brains are active and aware while processing and evaluating stimuli. It is in the beta cycle that we deal with problem solving and are engaged in the decision-making process. It is here that we are fully awake and cognizant.

The next cycle of the brain is called alpha. In alpha, our frequency of vibration slows down, and we begin to relax our mind. Alpha state is the state in which we daydream and are able to block out external stimuli that clutters our mind and keeps us on edge. Have you ever traveled in a car and missed your exit because you were lost in thought? Have you ever watched a movie and ignored the noise and distractions that might exist around you? If so, your brain was functioning in the cycle of alpha. In this cycle, because we are able to block out distractions, our mind becomes more open to the possibilities of creative ideas. Many people who are beginners at meditation easily learn to cycle down the frequency of their brain waves from beta to alpha and reach a relaxed state of body and mind.

A deeper cycle of the brain is called theta. In this state, we become even more capable of blocking out external distractions and slow our bodies down into an even greater state of relaxation. In the theta state, we are able to produce more vivid, detailed, and believable images of what we desire, thus becoming enabled to write a more convincing program into our subconscious mind.

Experiencing the theta cycle of the mind is much like the way you feel when you wake from sleep. It is a deep, lucid state of focused awareness. In this state, our mind becomes even more open to suggestion and our ability to reshape our belief system is enhanced. With practice in relaxation, we are all capable of reaching this deep and potent state of consciousness.

The final cycle of the brain is delta. In this state, we are asleep. There are numerous theories regarding the power of suggestion as we sleep and the messages we receive through dreams. Although there exists much discussion regarding this issue, the one undisputed fact regarding the sleep state of delta is that it offers our body the opportunity to rest and revitalize our energy.

<u>Mental Exercise:</u>

There are numerous theories regarding how to bring your consciousness into these deeper realms of relaxation. The one that is most effective in helping you reach these desired states is the one that works best for you. Just as food, clothing, and interests are all personal choices, so is the method of thought that delivers you into a deeper state of consciousness. What matters most is that you develop an understanding of why it is beneficial to reach these cycles of the brain and the most effective method or methods to get you there. As you practice entering these states of awareness, it becomes easier and quicker to achieve your desired level of relaxation. The following is an example of one exercise I use to help clients deepen their state of relaxation.

Find a comfortable place to sit and allow yourself to relax. Take a few relaxing breaths and begin to pay attention to your breathing. Feel the breath go in and out of your body, easily and effortlessly.

Next, take a deep breath and allow it to travel all the way to your abdomen. Hold it there briefly for a moment, then exhale through your mouth. Do this once more—a deep breath in, allow the air to travel all the way down into your abdomen, hold it briefly, and then exhale through your mouth. Do this one more time, and feel your body relax as you do so. As you inhale, imagine a relaxing and healing energy entering your body. As you exhale, imagine all stress, tension, and anxiety being released from your being.

Now focus your attention on the top of your head. Feel your temple beginning to relax. Follow this feeling of relaxation down into your eyes. Allow your eyes to feel very relaxed until they gently close. Continue to feel this relaxed feeling as it sinks lower into your facial area. Feel your cheeks, your tongue, and your jaw going into a comfortable state of relaxation.

Next, allow this relaxing feeling to travel down your neck, relaxing the muscles that support you. Imagine this relaxed feeling traveling through both shoulders, relaxing them deeply as they become heavier. Feel this relaxing sensation traveling down your arms, relaxing your muscles—your biceps and triceps—and your elbows, forearms, wrists, and fingers. Feel totally relaxed and wonderful.

Now shift your focus to the muscles of your chest and your back. Feel these muscles begin to become heavy and relaxed, creating a comfortable sensation. Feel your back melting into the object on which you are sitting. You are feeling so relaxed, so carefree.

Allow this sinking and comfortable feeling to enter your pelvic area and begin to slide down your legs. Feel the quadriceps and hamstrings become heavy with relaxation; allow this sensation to pass through your knees, your ankles, and all the way down to the tips of your toes. Just sit for a moment, and feel your body totally immersed in relaxation.

Now, using your imagination, become aware of the numbers 10, 9, 8, 7, 6, 5, 4, 3, 2, 1 before you. In your imagination, place a circle around each. Next, still using your imagination, erase each number, one at a time. As you erase each number, you go even deeper and deeper into relaxation. As you erase the number 1, take another deep, relaxing breath, and simply be still. Remain in this stillness for as long as you wish. It is a place of total comfort and total safety. Empty your mind of all active thoughts. Just relax and be still.

Begin now:

- *10...erase*

- *9....erase*

- *8...erase...becoming more relaxed*

- *7...erase*

- *6...erase...deeper into relaxation*

- *5...erase*

- *4...erase...much deeper*

- *3...erase*

- *2...erase...deeper and deeper into relaxation*

- *1...erase...completely relaxed and still*

When you feel your mind becoming active once again, imagine the numbers 1, 2, 3, 4, and 5 before you. Once again, with your imagination, erase each number, and as you do so, feel yourself become more active. You begin to sense the article on which you are seated and the familiarity and vibration of the room. When you reach the number 5, open your eyes being fully present, relaxed, and feeling so very comfortable.

The more you practice going into the state of deep relaxation, the more easily and quickly you will attain this state of consciousness. Like all acquired skills, practice and persistence will yield more effective results. The above model is a very effective exercise to use; however, there are many other techniques that work just as well. It is a good idea to explore different relaxation exercises or even create exercises of your own. The most effective vehicles for attaining a relaxed state of mind are the ones that work best for you. Do not focus so much on the vehicle of delivery; focus on the destination. Arriving at a deep and relaxed state of mind offers you a number of physical, mental, and emotional benefits. It is from the state of relaxation that your subconscious mind can be reprogrammed to create a new system of beliefs that will create the outcomes you truly desire in your life.

The tool of relaxation is effective and powerful. Learn to use the power of your imagination to help to create the results and successes that you truly desire.

Eleven

Seven Steps toward Manifestation

If you can really, really see it, you can really, really be it!

Step #1: VISUALIZATION

All dreams and goals begin first in the mind. We have all had fantasies and daydreams of things we would like to do or have in our life. We would become excited and see how our lives would change dramatically only to have our fantasies and excitement diminished by the "realistic" thoughts of why we could never make our dreams come true. We then redirect our thoughts in a new direction, leaving our great ideas behind.

A vision differs from a fantasy. A vision is something we can actually see ourselves accomplishing; a vision is something that resonates within us; a vision is tangible and real. If you can really, really see it, you can really, really be it.

Visualization was explained in an earlier chapter of this book; it is a powerful tool that works best by attaching as much sensory input as possible to whatever it is that you can see. The most effective way to visualize is to begin at the end and work your way back to the beginning. The more you can actually see, feel, hear, taste, touch, and smell the end result of your vision, the more powerful the vision becomes. Creating a clear, concise vision of what you truly want to become manifest in your life is the first step toward accomplishing a goal and making your dream come true. The more real and powerful the vision becomes, the greater the likelihood that you will accomplish whatever it is that you can truly see.

Step #2: DESIRE

Desire is the emotion that provides the fuel you need to achieve your chosen goal and make that dream come true. Merely wishing for something sends out a weak signal to the subconscious mind, which in turn will conduct a weak search for ways to act upon the idea. However, as your vision becomes more real in your mind, your desire will increase proportionately. As your desire increases, you are signaling your mind to search in earnest for ways to make your vision become a reality. When you reach the point where your desire begins to burn within you, then you have reached the point of focusing on ways to succeed and become empowered to push aside thoughts of doubt, fear, and failure. Create a fire within yourself, and you will create the energy of success.

Step #3: BELIEF

Belief is another key element in accomplishing your goals and making your dreams come true. Once your mind creates a vivid vision of what you want and you feel a burning desire to pursue it, believing that it can actually take place is the next step toward manifesting it in your life. When you truly believe in your ability to create what you visualize and desire, then you truly become empowered to succeed. When you truly believe in your ability to succeed, your mind will think in terms of possibilities rather than limitations. Your mind will then become more comfortable in thinking thoughts that are positive and less comfortable entertaining thoughts that are negative. Your inner dialogue will change as well. You will eliminate self-talk that implies "I can't" and replace it with self-talk that speaks in terms of "I can." If you think you can succeed, you might, and then again, you might not. When you *believe* you will succeed, then somehow, some way, you will.

Step #4: FAITH

Faith is the next step toward accomplishing your goals and making your dreams come true. Faith is the intrinsic knowledge that what you see, desire, and believe will become manifested in your life. It is that intuitive part of your mind that tells you not to worry, that encourages you to keep your dreams alive because if you do so, then somehow, some way, they actually will become real. Faith is the intangible power that tells you that you will succeed; it is your "inner knower" that you learn to know intimately and trust. Faith creates within you the feeling that all is well. Faith is the stuff that moves mountains; it is the power that transforms insurmountable obstacles into hurdles that can be overcome; it is the deep-rooted intuitive part of yourself that tells you that the dreams you are dreaming are actually coming true.

<u>Step #5</u>: A PLAN

Creating a vision, desire, and belief and having faith are powerful steps toward manifestation; however, they will remain dormant if you do not develop a plan for how to accomplish your goal or make your dreams come true. Without a plan, you remain in the state of fantasy.

Once you develop a plan of action, you are then ready to transform your dream into reality. Like visualization, the more specific and detailed your plan, the more you will encourage your subconscious mind to search for ways to draw your goal or dream toward you. Our mind works in pictures; when a stimulus is presented to us, we form a mental picture in our mind's eye. For some, it is not a visual "seeing"; it may present itself in the form of a feeling, but nevertheless, a stimulus will create a type of visual response within us. Developing a clear and vivid image of what you truly desire will create more certainty within you. The more certainty you create within you, the more easily the steps you need to make your dream come true will unfold before you.

With a well-defined plan in place, you become empowered to transform fantasy into reality. Keep in mind that your plan of action needs to be flexible; it may require revisions as you proceed along the way. Consider the example of hiring a contractor to build a home for you. You create a clear and concise blueprint, and construction begins. However, as the structure becomes shaped, you may decide you would like to alter plans you did not see specifically or clearly in the original blueprint. You discuss this with your contractor and make the appropriate changes. The same is true for your action plan. Begin by creating a "blueprint." Write it down, and study it. Revise it as many times as needed to begin "construction" of your goal and dream. You are free to make alterations along the way as your mind discovers new and better ways to proceed. However, keep this statement in mind: without a plan for making it come true, a vision is just a fantasy. Plan for success, and it will be yours to enjoy.

<u>Step #6</u>: ACTION

You now have a clear vision, a great desire, a belief that you can accomplish this goal, faith that you will do so, and a concise plan. However, the state of fantasy still exists if you fail to take action. If you wait for others to come knocking at your door, it is likely you will be waiting for a very long time! There are those who have great ideas and wait for opportunity to knock at their door, and there are those who have great ideas who go out and do the knocking. Who do you suppose will be more likely to succeed? You must take action toward making your dream become a reality.

The first step toward making your dream a reality is often the most difficult because you are moving beyond the safety of your comfort zone. However, once you place your foot on the path toward making your dream become a reality, the journey toward manifestation actually begins.

I had a client who desired to create a change in his physical appearance through nutrition and exercise. He had attempted to do so several times on his own but was unable to sustain any form of successful regimen. He knew he needed assistance and began to search for someone to help him. Afterward, he told me he had discovered an advertisement I had placed in a local publication and considered calling, but his procrastination prevented him from making the telephone call. However, my client found himself constantly returning to that advertisement and one day finally picked up the telephone and made the call. He arrived at my office on the appointed day half an hour early and sat in his car attempting to summon the courage to actually come to the door. He finally convinced himself to step beyond his comfort zone and rang the doorbell. Once the door opened and he stepped beyond the threshold, a new perception began to shape his thoughts and an entirely new set of beliefs, certainty, and transition began to take place within his mind. The end result was that a new level of performance and a healthier and happier lifestyle became established in his life. All it really took was taking that first step to set him on the path toward accomplishing his goal and making his dream a reality. The same can be true for you as well; take action and make your dream come true.

Step #7: PERSISTENCE

You now have a clear vision, a strong desire, belief, and faith that you will succeed; you have created a concise plan and have taken action. The final step toward achieving your goal and making your dream come true is persistence.

In a perfect world, perfecting the first six steps would lead you to manifestation in a smooth and easy manner; however, life is not always a perfect experience. For many of us, there are constant twists, turns, and bumps along the road. Success can sometimes be a difficult and arduous journey, but if you persist in pursuing your dream, then somehow, some way, it will become your reality. I have known many successful people, and one common trait they all possess is that they persist in their beliefs; they never give up on what they believe will come true. Continue to look forward; you cannot change your former behaviors and mistakes; it is unwise to dwell on the past to the point where it becomes detrimental to your future. You cannot change your past; however, you have the ability to create your future. Use your past failures or disappointments to motivate you to change for the better, not to continue feeling bad about yourself.

The world is filled with stories about people who were told they could never accomplish what their hearts and minds told them that they could. These are people who proceeded with the perception that setbacks are not failures; setbacks are really valuable opportunities to take a step back and revise their plan of action regarding how to move forward once again in a more efficient and effective manner. These are people who have kept their eye on the prize as their life evolved into the reality they had created within their minds. Surrendering is easier than persisting through difficult and discouraging moments in time; unfortunately, the regrets of surrender may linger within a person for a very long time. Persevering is often difficult through the arduous and discouraging moments of life's adversities; however, the rewards of success prevail within a person for a very long time as well. Your goals and dreams may require that you reshape and reform them many times during the course of the journey, but if you persevere and pursue your dreams, your mind will find a way of making them come true. The vision spawned within the imagination of your mind can and will become the reality that you live. Never surrender the dream that lives within your heart, no matter how long it takes it to materialize. Don't just dare to dream; dare to make your dream come true.

Twelve

The Meaning of Life

A seeker of truth had heard of a great and wise master who lived high in the mountains of a remote corner of the earth. It was said in many circles of the world that this wise man knew of life's most precious secret, that he carried within him the answer to the true meaning of life.

The seeker was not a man of particular means, and he had struggled within himself almost all of his life. He had tried in earnest, and often in vain, to find a sense of peace and happiness within his mind and heart. When he was told of this wise man, who dwelled in a faraway place, the seeker knew, he simply knew, that he must somehow, someway, stand in this wise man's presence and have the true meaning of life revealed to him.

This being so, the seeker researched thoroughly just how he could reach this wise man. He sold his possessions, gathered his modest belongings, and set out on the arduous and unfamiliar journey. He began his quest with a light heart and a spirit of purpose knowing that he would be traveling a great distance and that it would challenge him physically, mentally, and emotionally. However, there was no trip so difficult, no hardship so harsh that it could deter him from his quest. He envisioned his journey as the proverbial rainbow whose reward was the mythical pot of gold that lay just beyond the rainbow's edge. In his mind, this precious pot of gold represented wisdom; the wise man was the purveyor of this magnificent treasure.

The seeker journeyed with enthusiasm, and despite the numerous obstacles that presented themselves along the way, neither time nor distance diminished his spirit. He regarded each step he took as a step toward discovering life's sacred truth.

Reaching the foothills of his destination, the seeker paused and reflected upon the challenges he had experienced along his journey. He suddenly felt a great rush of energy enter his body, and it propelled his feet to move forward quickly, defying the fatigue and hardships he had overcome to reach this moment in time. He ascended the mountain and navigated the wooded terrain with catlike precision. Although he was unfamiliar with the mountain's character, he instinctively knew where to step, where to turn. He simply knew.

When he arrived upon the mountain's summit, he paused to survey the magnificence of the landscape below. He stood quietly for a long moment and reflected upon how far he had traveled. The difficulty of moments past dissolved into nothingness. His silent trance was suddenly interrupted by a sound that drifted from somewhere beyond his field of vision. It was a rich, full, and sweet sound that he heard. It was a happy sound. The seeker knew this sound could be emanating from only one source. The beautiful, sweet, humming sound of a rhythmic melody was coming from the master.

The seeker moved forward with light footsteps, for he wanted to be careful not to startle the master, yet his steps were heavy enough to announce his arrival. He knew no words to speak; he allowed the reverence of his footsteps to speak the words his mind could not properly convey.

Stepping into a clearing, he saw him. There, sitting on a seat fashioned from the stump of a tree, was the master. The master's gaze remained fixed on the mountain's edge, as if he were mesmerized by the view of the valley that lay beyond and below. The seeker stood motionless, not knowing how to address him. The master's gentle voice pierced the silence. Keeping his gaze toward the valley, he uttered, "Welcome, my friend. I hope that your eyes are aware of the great beauty that my eyes behold. Do you see what I see?"

The muscles of his arms and legs suddenly relaxed, which seemed to release the torrents of tension that his anticipation had created in his mind. The master's simple greeting prompted him to recall the words he had rehearsed to himself a thousand times before. Moving three steps closer to the wise man, he spoke softly. "Great Master, I have traveled a long distance to be here in this moment, in this place, in the presence of one of whom people of the world speak with great respect and reverence. I have sold my possessions and left my home to find you. I have come to you with a heart filled with hope, and all I request is that you answer a question that has burned within me for my entire lifetime."

The master remained motionless, his gaze still focused on the valley. The seeker felt his body becoming rigid as he awaited the anticipated response. The silence, which seemed eternal, was finally broken. "I am happy to have you in my company. You are a welcomed guest to my home. Now, knowing that you have journeyed long and far to seek my company, it will be my true pleasure to address your question. Tell me, my friend, what might your question be?"

The seeker began, "Great Master, I have only one question to ask, and it is my fervent wish that your response will fulfill my lifelong desire to know. It is a question I have pondered over and over again since the days of my childhood. I have found no true peace within my mind or soul because each time I think I have unraveled this great mystery of life, I find myself in doubt that the answer that I have derived is true. So, Great Master, it is said that you are the one living spirit on this earth who understands life's true meaning. I ask only that you reveal to me the secret to living a full, happy, and peaceful life."

The seeker fixed his gaze upon the master's eyes as the master turned toward him. In these eyes that had become fixed upon him was the look of true wisdom and understanding; in these eyes that were fixed upon him, the seeker recognized benevolence. In these eyes that were fixed upon him, the seeker recognized truth. The muscles in his chest and abdomen tightened, causing his breath to cease as he awaited the reply he had journeyed so long and so far to have revealed to him. He stood in a motionless trance as the master formulated his reply.

The master returned his gaze to the valley, seemingly searching for the proper words to form in his mind. The seeker's confidence began to soar in anticipation of his life's mission finally being completed. His moment of truth had finally arrived. He continued holding his breath as the master turned his head toward him once again.

"My friend, you have asked the age-old question. It is a question that has been asked by many who have walked this earth before you. It is a question being asked in every corner of the world as we speak in this moment. It is a question that will be asked again and again even after you and I have completed our life upon this earth and have moved into other realms of spirit. It is a question that has mystified man since his inception. I will simplify my answer so you can understand the true meaning of life and be filled with a spirit of renewed energy and purpose."

The seeker became aware of the beads of perspiration that had formed on his forehead. He leaned forward as he exhaled the breath that had remained pent up inside of him. The master spoke: "My friend, the simplest explanation I can offer you in this moment is this: life is simply a bowl of cherries."

The master allowed his gaze to rest upon the seeker's face for a moment longer and then turned his head back toward the valley below.

The seeker's body once again tightened. He leaned forward, straining to hear what would be said to him next. The silence became so unbearable that he could no longer contain himself. He cried out, "Please, Great Master, tell me more! I ask you once again, with the greatest respect and reverence that my heart can hold. Please, Great Master, what is the true answer? What is the true meaning of life?"

The master returned his gaze toward the traveler. His words were soft, not much louder than a whisper.

"That is all that needs to be said, my friend. Life is simply a bowl of cherries."

The seeker's eyes narrowed, his posture becoming erect. He stared hard at the master who sat motionlessly before him. He realized that the master's words were final. He sprang forward suddenly, narrowing the distance between them. He felt the wave of redness that spread rapidly across his face as he blurted, "That is it? Life is a bowl of cherries? Is this your great and wise secret? I have planned this trip for years, sold my possessions, spent great sums of money, endured hardships and countless obstacles to arrive in this remote corner of the earth seeking your deepest insights about the true meaning of life, and all I have heard from you is, 'Life is a bowl of cherries!' This is the wisdom of the one who is considered to be the wisest of all men in this world!"

The lines on the master's face softened, and his eyes reflected a deep resonance of peace.

"This is what I wish to reveal to you regarding the secret of life, my friend. Very simply, life is truly a bowl of cherries. Now, you have traveled a long way and invested much time and money to find me; therefore, there is one more thought I wish to discuss with you—"

The seeker's hands clenched and unclenched several times. His stomach cramped into tight knots, and his jaw tightened as his mind searched to focus on the thoughts that raced through his consciousness. Finally, he bellowed, "I cannot believe I have allowed myself to be deceived by a foolish old man who sits high on a hill, pretending to be a wise and profound teacher of truth! Be gone with you, old man. I cannot believe I have permitted myself to be such a stupid and ignorant fool! There is not a single thing you can tell me that I would waste any more of my valuable time and energy upon. It is my life's deepest regret that I have invested so much of my energy and my very soul thinking that an old man could teach me the true meaning of life. Life is a bowl of cherries! I am such an incredible fool!"

The seeker whirled around and headed for the path that led down the steep mountain. The cracking of the underbrush created by his heavy footsteps echoed like thunder, reflecting the anger that had welled up inside of him.

The master's smile did not fade, and his eyes remained soft as his gaze followed the seeker. When he was lost from his sight, the master listened patiently as the sound of the seeker's footsteps gradually faded into the distance. When they had faded into silence, he returned his gaze to the valley below. He chuckled softly to himself, knowing his message would be understood by the seeker at the proper moment in time. All things occur in the moment they are meant to. His wisdom was not lost on the seeker; it would simply take time for his understanding to take place. The master heaved a heavy sigh as he thought for a moment of how things might have been a bit easier for the seeker to comprehend had he allowed him to complete his message. He wished to tell him that yes, life is a bowl of cherries, but it can also be a barrel of sour grapes. It all depends on how you perceive it.

In the simplest terms, the wise master's message is this: life is what you believe it to be. It is simply a matter of how you choose to perceive it. Happiness and fulfillment are not the products of circumstance; they are the products of the thoughts you choose to entertain in your mind.

Wishing you Peace, Love, and a Smile in your Heart!

About the Authors

Glenn Poveromo is a man of many interests and experiences that have guided him on his journey to create The Power of Visualization. His career as a teacher and inter-scholastic coach has provided him with innumerable opportunities to teach and motivate literally thousands of young men and women to improve their lives.

Glenn has always possessed a keen interest in how the positive mind is able to influence positive outcomes in life. Because of this interest he studied many aspects of awareness which include physical, mental, and spiritual modalities. He is a graduate of Southern Connecticut State University and received his Masters Degree in Special Education from CW Post College. He also received his certification as a member of the National Guild of Hypnotists at the Tribecca Institute in Manhattan, has studied "The Winner's Mentality" with the former trainer of the New York Jets, Bob Reese, and has studied with Gary Parks of the 3E Institute in Huntington, NY.

Glenn and his wife, Sheri, have spent years developing their current program which offers insights and exercises that can easily be understood and implemented by anyone who seeks to enhance all arenas of life. They conduct individual and group sessions, as well as seminars and lectures.

Glenn is the author of *The Spirit's Self-Help Book* and also sends his *Glennisms: Simple Thoughts About Life and Living* to thousands of people throughout the world each Monday, Wednesday, and Friday. To learn more about his book and Glennisms, visit his web site at: www.thepov.net. You can contact Glenn via email at: creatingstrength@aol.com.

Dr. Jessie Poveromo is a firm believer in the notion that people can train themselves to think better in order to feel better and she utilizes this philosophy in both her personal and professional life. Jessie is a New York state licensed psychologist and a partner at New York Cognitive Therapy and Wellness Center, where she provides cognitive behavioral therapy to adolescents, adults, and the elderly who may be experiencing depression, anxiety disorders, personality disorders, and body image issues. She received her bachelor's degree in psychology from the University of Delaware and went on to receive both her masters and doctoral degrees from Hofstra University. Dr. Poveromo trained in both inpatient and outpatient mental health settings and has provided services to several Long Island school districts. Her research interests include media effects on body dissatisfaction and how social comparison contributes to body image distortion. Jessie lives in New York with her family. You can find more information on Jessie's private practice at NewYorkCognitive.com

Made in the USA
Charleston, SC
06 November 2011